JOHN KNILL'S NAVY

Five Years on the Cut

Sir John Knill

CANALBOOKSHOP

JOHN KNILL'S NAVY

Five Years on the Cut

Sir John Knill

First edition 1998
published by the author

Second edition 2020
CanalBookShop
Audlem Mill Limited The Wharf Audlem Cheshire CW3 0DX
www.canalbookshop.co.uk

Printed in the UK

ISBN 978-1-9160125-2-3

CONTENTS

Tom Rolt, author of *Narrow Boat*, which book prompted the formation of the Inland Waterways Association in 1946, and the subsequent canal revival.

FOREWORD TO FIRST EDITION

by the late Sonia Rolt

I am honoured to be asked to give the Foreword to this remarkable book, this unique memoir. Because I appear in its pages from time to time as one of the quite small band of those active on the canals over the period described, I thought I might be prejudiced in its favour. Indeed I am, if recognition of what has been achieved, by a remarkable feat of memory, to enlighten and inform, is the criteria.

Sir John must be the only protagonist/owner of working boats of the time who ran them successfully, with the ups and downs of trading and maintenance, during the rapidly changing post-war scene. In addition, he has also contrived, by powerful descriptions of the working operation of boats and locks and by the warmth of his evocation of all the boat people and others who impinged on the towpath or in dim-lit London rooms on his deeply committed activities of the time, to give readers a vivid feeling as well as the images of a wholly vanished world.

I remember the glowing red of *Columba* and *Uranus* so graphically described by Sir John that you can almost taste it, even though what I had to compare it with, at the time and in memory, is a newly-docked wooden butty boat of the Samuel Barlow Coal Carrying Company sliding out from the dry dock at Braunston, with all the glory of red and green and oak graining; lakes and bridges, castles and flowering bunched roses, white, yellow, brown and purple glitteringly reflected in the dark waters of the cut. Sir John's two boats were of a slightly more severe, one might say naval, style, but in the talented hands of Dave Clark at Nursers Yard conformed to this definitive and matchless standard.

I write as if all Sir John's involvements were in the past. This is far from the case. He is markedly involved and has remained so with energy, advice and thought, which is shown by the positions of trust and authority he occupies in canal societies.

In conclusion, this book should be read by anyone who asks and comes to wonder just how he, or she, has arrived in this surviving, incomparable secret and watery world.

Sonia Rolt
Stanley Pontlarge
Gloucestershire
1998

INTRODUCTION TO SECOND EDITION

Looking back at the last hurrah of Britain's canals just after the Second World War, from the perspective of today's landscape, seems like an insight into a remarkable world.

The railways have been recognised as being important where natural resources have to be husbanded and the environment protected.

It is ironic that reopening lines closed during a period of postwar austerity is now the answer to today's pollution & congestion.

Not so for the canals, where their value seems to lie in offering recreation for people who enjoy or want to experience boating and the country side.

Will our world, society and economy change so much that one day, water transport in this country becomes a viable consideration?

For the moment at least, my father's book offers a firsthand insight into a way of life that has vanished, and where the past truly seems like another country.

Tom Knill
Pembridge
Herefordshire
July 2020

Publisher's note to second edition, 2020

Knowing that people have been trying to hunt down secondhand copies of *John Knill's Navy* that probably did not exist, CanalBookShop approached the family as copyright owner for permission to reprint the book, which has been granted.

The opportunity has been taken to correct a few errors, and modern digital print processes allow the inclusion of many more illustrations, most of which might have been seen elsewhere, but they are brought together here for the first time.

I would like to thank the late Sir John Knill's sons Jenkyn and Tom for their help and guidance in putting this volume together, and also David Jowett, who performed the same task with the first edition, for providing scans of many of the photos.

Peter Silvester
CanalBookShop
Audlem Mill
July 2020

INTRODUCTION TO FIRST EDITION

How did this book come to be written?

In the late 1970s, I gave an interview to a student from Southampton University, which was taped. Some years later, I was sent a copy of the tape which arrived after my wife had died.

I was particularly pleased to receive it, because I discovered that my late wife's voice was on it. She had made comments during the interview; it was as if she was in the room again.

I played the tape to a friend, Ivor Bryant, and asked for his comments. He thought that it would make the basis for a good book, so Ivor set to work. As explained in the book, I had destroyed my logs in 1955, so I had to search my memory, so here after many vicissitudes is some of the story of John Knill's Navy.

Sir John Knill
Bathampton
March 1998

ABOUT THE AUTHOR

John Knill was born in 1913 in Blackheath, London, and educated at Downside School in Stretton-on-the-Fosse in Somerset. He was called up to the Royal Naval Volunteer Supplementary Reserve in 1939 and then to the Royal Naval Volunteer Reserve in 1940. He saw action in home waters, in the Mediterranean, and in Normandy during the D Day landings, before being demobilised as Lieutenant RNVR in 1945.

He bought a pair of working boats and became involved in the secluded world of the canals, a world he describes in the pages of this book. This led to him serving on the Council of the infant Inland Waterways Association.

During his canal carrying days he married Martin Barnes and they had two sons, Tom in 1952 and Jenkyn in 1954. After leaving the canals behind in 1954, the family moved to Herefordshire to farm until 1963.

Moving off in another direction, John Knill became a Civil Servant in international naval sales, a position he held until 1977.

John Knill became Sir John when he succeeded to the Baronetcy at the time of his father's death in 1973.

In 1967 the family had moved to Bathampton, near Bath on the Kennet & Avon Canal. A successful trip boat operation was started in the early 1970s on the isolated navigable section before the canal was fully restored.

Sir John Knill's wife Martin died in 1983.

Sir John was President of the Commercial Narrowboat Operators Association and President of the Association of Canal Enterprises - Kennet & Avon, (founded by his wife).

He was Vice President of the Cotswold Canals Trust, the Hereford & Gloucester Canal Trust and the Wilts & Berks Canal Trust, all organisations in the process of restoring canals.

Sir John was an Honorary Life Member of the Inland Waterways Association and in addition was President of Avon Transport 2000.

Sir John Knill died in 1998.

David Jowett

ACKNOWLEDGEMENTS

I have spent hours thinking about acknowledgements; I hope that I have not left anybody out.

My thanks to Ivor Bryant who helped me from the start and whose idea it really was. Thanks for the 80,000 words that he typed. My thanks also to the late Christopher Marsh (Division Waterways Officer, North West Division of the Docks & Inland Waterways Executive), for offering to read and comment on the original manuscript.

To the volunteers of the Hereford & Gloucester Canal Trust for all the work that they did, especially for committing the manuscript to computer disc. To the late Tom Rolt who helped me in the early days and gave me his friendship, and to Sonia Rolt who gave me encouragement and friendship when we were boating, and more recently with the production of this book. Thanks also to Sonia for the permission to quote from *Narrow Boat*. To the late Jack Gashion and the late Robert Longden for their photographs.

To the crews who gave me their friendship and loyalty, Jim Jackson, Joe Hill, Fred Hobbs, Tom Foxon, the late Bob Pettifer, the late Ray White, Don Rosenburg, Wally James, the late Alf Best, Ron Wilson, the late Lawrence Grantham and their families who were all so kind to me, the late John Hemelryk and all those other boatmen who helped me on my way and did so much to encourage me and to improve my boating and taught me to "git them paddles up".

To Edward Paget-Tomlinson for allowing me to use his painting depicting the livery of my boats from his series *Colours of the Cut* serialised in Waterways World (July 1989 issue).

To my Mother, Grandmother and my Wife for their love and unfailing support, and not to be forgotten, Bosun for his devotion and friendship and the hundreds of miles his little legs must have carried him when accompanying me lock-wheeling, all of which contributed to the pleasures and memories of *John Knill's Navy*.

And finally, to David Jowett for getting *John Knill's Navy* into shape for publishing.

Sir John Knill
Bathampton
March 1998

John Knill, standing by the (then) relatively new Ham Baker paddle gear on a mid-1930s build Grand Union lock.

Jim Jackson

Columba's engine 'ole

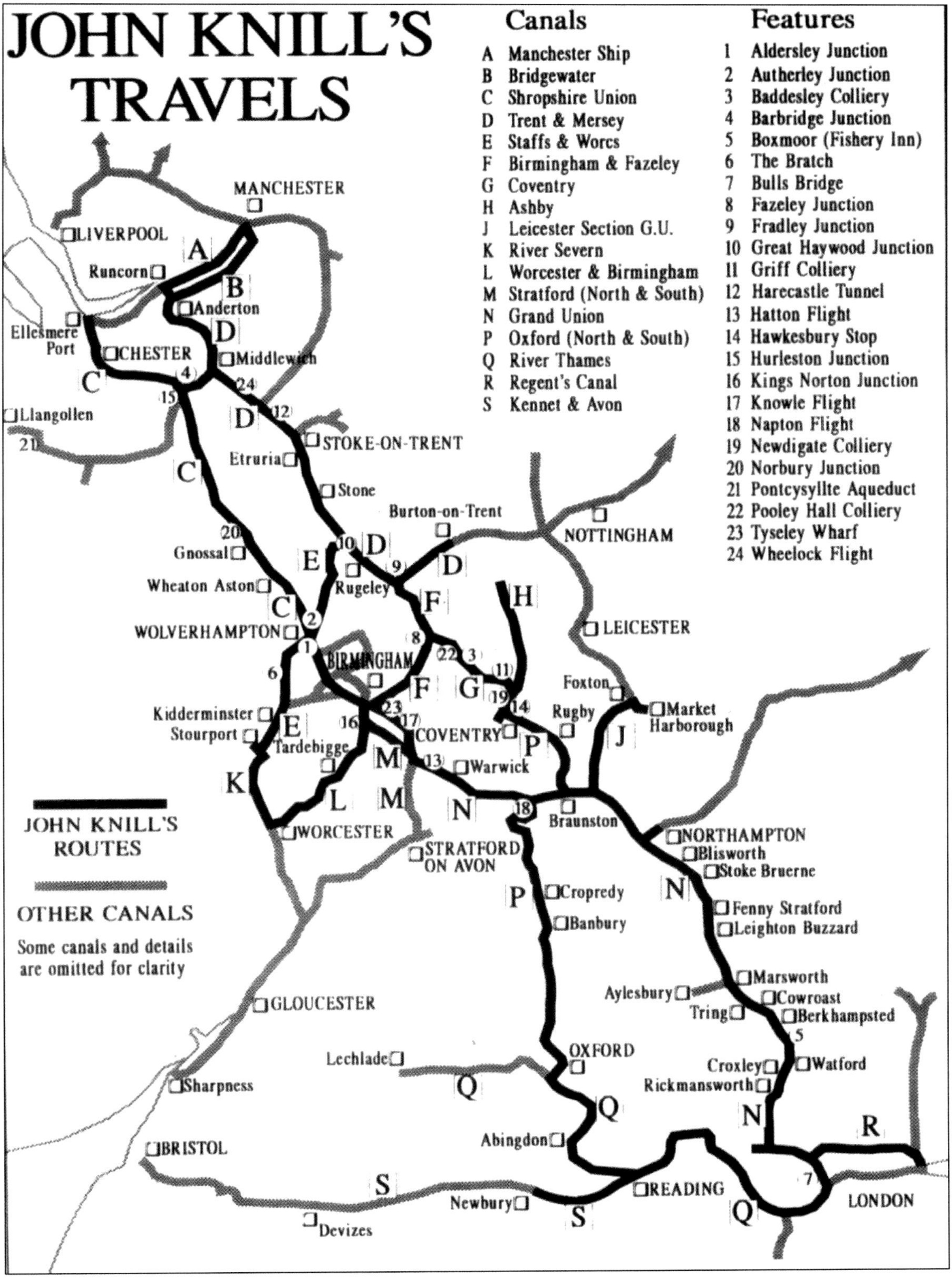
JOHN KNILL'S TRAVELS
Canals
A Manchester Ship
B Bridgewater
C Shropshire Union
D Trent & Mersey
E Staffs & Worcs
F Birmingham & Fazeley
G Coventry
H Ashby
J Leicester Section G.U.
K River Severn
L Worcester & Birmingham
M Stratford (North & South)
N Grand Union
P Oxford (North & South)
Q River Thames
R Regent's Canal
S Kennet & Avon
Features
1 Aldersley Junction
2 Autherley Junction
3 Baddesley Colliery
4 Barbridge Junction
5 Boxmoor (Fishery Inn)
6 The Bratch
7 Bulls Bridge
8 Fazeley Junction
9 Fradley Junction
10 Great Haywood Junction
11 Griff Colliery
12 Harecastle Tunnel
13 Hatton Flight
14 Hawkesbury Stop
15 Hurleston Junction
16 Kings Norton Junction
17 Knowle Flight
18 Napton Flight
19 Newdigate Colliery
20 Norbury Junction
21 Pontcysyllte Aqueduct
22 Pooley Hall Colliery
23 Tyseley Wharf
24 Wheelock Flight
MANCHESTER
LIVERPOOL
Runcorn
Anderton
Ellesmere Port
CHESTER
Middlewich
Llangollen
STOKE-ON-TRENT
Etruria
Stone
Burton-on-Trent
NOTTINGHAM
Gnossal
Wheaton Aston
Rugeley
WOLVERHAMPTON
BIRMINGHAM
LEICESTER
Foxton
Market Harborough
Kidderminster
Stourport
Tardebigge
COVENTRY
Rugby
Warwick
WORCESTER
STRATFORD ON AVON
Braunston
NORTHAMPTON
Blisworth
Stoke Bruerne
Cropredy
Banbury
Fenny Stratford
Leighton Buzzard
GLOUCESTER
Aylesbury
Marsworth
Cowroast
Tring
Berkhampsted
Lechlade
OXFORD
Croxley
Watford
Sharpness
Rickmansworth
Abingdon
BRISTOL
READING
Newbury
LONDON
Devizes
JOHN KNILL'S ROUTES
OTHER CANALS
Some canals and details are omitted for clarity

My first trip to Hawkesbury in 1948. The photograph above formed the basis of one of IWA's Christmas Cards in 1997 (below). *Columba* and *Uranus* are still painted in the colours of the previous owners H Dean & Sons. Photo, above: Robert Longden. Oil painting, below: Harley Crossley.

Columba at Sutton's (Hawkesbury Junction). **Above**: in 1948 - the first coal run, turning on to the Coventry Canal. *Columba* is still in H. Dean & Son's grey livery with yellow lettering. **Below**: Rounding the junction, not helped by a sticky valve, with John Knill steering. The boat in front of the Greyhound pub is Joe Skinner's *Friendship*. Photos: Robert Longden.

Chapter One

MY START

How did it all start? For me, I suppose, it began in 1918, the year of my fifth birthday. My father used to take a magazine called *Transport and Travel Monthly* which covered every form of transport from railways and the sea to ballooning. There were articles in it on canals, and I remember an illustration that particularly took my fancy. It was a picture of a three-way bridge on a canal. The railway was underneath, then the canal, and then the road going over the top - all crossing over at the same point. For many years I remembered that bridge.

The next thing I remember, as far as canals are concerned, was some time in about 1925 or 1926; going up to Knill in Herefordshire from Sussex we passed round the edge of a hill and saw a great flight of locks rising up above us, with all the balance beams painted white. For many years I could not identify this; then, on a cycle trip up the Kennet and Avon Canal which I relate in Chapter Three, I immediately recognised the scene as soon as I set eyes on the Devizes Flight with its locks and adjacent side-pounds.

In 1932 I went to live in Wimbledon. Browsing in a second-hand bookshop one day, I happened to find a copy of *Bradshaw's Guide to the Inland Waterways*. This instantly took my fancy, not because I was particularly interested in canals, but because I had always been interested in this kind of publication, whether it dealt with ships, railways, cars, or what have you. I bought it for six shillings (30p) and quite honestly forgot all about it. I never had any need to refer to it in any way, as I just had no contact with canals.

Then 1940 came, I joined the Navy and was away from 1940 to 1945. In 1945 I returned from sea to Sheerness as Assistant Gunnery Officer, 21st Destroyer Flotilla, and one of my jobs was to run the Liberty Boat Service. Eventually we had in all about eight large 36 foot motor launches, five large harbour launches (two steam and three diesel), and various other craft as well. We had 120 petty officers, sailors and motor mechanics to man this little flotilla, divided into two watches. Also, built up over a period of months, we had our own workshop in the coach houses of Admiralty House for repairs and maintenance. We never failed to bring in the men from sea as soon as the ships came into harbour from their patrol work and convoy duty.

When I was demobbed in 1945, I had the idea of using this knowledge of boats I had obtained to get myself an interesting job. I wrote to Thames Launches (Meres, as they used to be) and offered myself as a sort of maintenance engineer or welfare worker - quoting in support of my application the experience I had had in looking after men and boats when I was with the destroyer flotilla. However, they wrote back and said, "No, thank you very much."

Then I got in touch with the Grand Union Canal Company and told them what I had been doing, and that I would like to join them as a welfare officer. I had a reply from them, but, they too said, "No, thank you very much. We've got no room for anybody at the moment." That seemed to be the end of a bright idea.

I then started working for a cousin of mine, Cuthbert Watts, who ran an old established business called T. J. Cooke and Son in Wolverhampton. They manufactured and distributed what is called door furniture - door handles, door knobs, finger plates, keyhole covers, letter boxes and the like, all of the highest quality. The firm had its own pattern maker and a foundry for casting. The material was metal - brass, bronze and copper - but not aluminium.

I was taken on the staff as an Assistant Factory Manager, but not doing any actual managing. Then the girl who had been responsible for doing the accounts left to get married, so I took over from her. I had never been much good at this kind of thing. After a while I got into the way of things, and did quite well for a few months. Then I found myself beginning to get everything wrong. The figures simply would not come out right. Into the bargain, I was getting terrible headaches and trouble with my eyes.

I went to the eye hospital in Wolverhampton for examination. They discovered that I had a natural squint. It was, in fact, a lateral squint of fourteen degrees and a vertical squint of eight degrees and the tests also showed that I suffered from interrupted vision. At the range at which you read an account book, that meant that I was putting the pounds down in the pence column (at a time when it was still pounds, shillings and pence, of course). So there was the reason for the difficulties of balancing the books and the cause of the headaches, but what to do about it? The specialist said, "You've got to change your job, preferably for something out-of-doors".

I therefore left Cuthbert Watts and returned to Wimbledon to the house where my mother and grandmother were living. By this time I had read Rolt's *Narrow Boat*; an old family friend had given me a copy of an early edition of Temple Thurston's *Flower of Gloster* and I had read Emma Smith's *Maiden's Trip*. I had even looked into that long-forgotten copy of Bradshaw. So, when looking through a trade paper one day I saw an advertisement offering a pair of narrow boats for sale, I decided to buy them.

Luckily, both my mother and grandmother thought this was a good idea. I say luckily because in fact my grandmother agreed to give me a small bridging loan to complete the purchase price of £1,600. I suppose a similar pair today (in 1998) would cost about £25,000. After seeing the boats I decided that I would be pleased to take an option on them. Of course the boats had to be surveyed and then insured.

Whilst this was being sorted out I went through that period of awful anticipation which I'm sure many people have had when, having decided to buy something and not having got all the money together or made all the final arrangements, you wonder if someone else will get there before you.

I was helped at this point by a naval friend. John Baynham (Commander RNVR) had been Gunnery Officer of the 21st Destroyer Flotilla when I served as Assistant Gunnery Officer. He now worked for Anderson, Green and Company (the insurance side of the Orient Line) and he handled the survey of the narrow boats, at Bulls Bridge, and their subsequent insurance. The company were very amused at insuring my two boats in the sum of one and a half thousand pounds; immediately before they had been busy dealing with the insurance of the *Orsova* for three and a quarter million pounds!

At last the formalities were complete, so now the motor boat *Columba* and its butty *Uranus*, awaiting in the boatyard at Bulls Bridge, were mine. They were standard Grand Union Canal boats: small Woolwich built by Messrs. Harland and Wolff at North Woolwich in 1935, with a composite hull, i.e. steel with an elm bottom. The motor boat was powered by an 18 horse-power National diesel and the previous owners had built a cabin on ahead of the engine room in the bottom of the boat, to the same height as the rear cabin, so that there was extra sleeping accommodation. This was absolute luxury as it meant that with a crew of three, each could have his own cabin.

As we were following the traditions of working boatman and working alongside men and women whose families had been on the cut for generations, perhaps a word about how they managed would not be out of place here. In the old days, from about 1840 that is, the tradition grew up among boatmen of taking their families around the country with them. This was partly because the wages that were paid did not encourage a man to live on his boat and pay for his keep there and also have a house ashore. Having the family on board also meant economy in wages. Whilst two people could run a pair of working boats, things went more smoothly if the Captain had not just one but two others on board. One of the three would look after the horse, one would get the locks ready and the third would steer. Only in this way could one keep any reasonable kind of timetable at all. As children from the age of seven or eight upwards were quite capable of coping with most of the work involved, it was obviously cheaper to use the members of one's own family than to employ other boatmen who had to be paid.

With a pair of boats in the days of the horse, there would have been the possibility of four cabins altogether. Traditionally, the husband had the responsibility for the leading boat, and the wife for the butty boat. So the rear cabin in the butty was the main living quarters. Here all the cooking, washing, and so on, were done by the wife and daughters, and here too, husband and wife and the younger children slept. In the bows, if there was a small cabin you would have a cross-bed for the younger children. The eldest of the children might use the forward or the aft cabin of the leading boat.

In the main cabin there was a bed-place that went right across the boat, and this folded out of a kind of cupboard. Then, on the right-hand side you would have a bed along the side of the boat which also served as a seat for meals. On the opposite side would be the range. The table hinged down from the cupboard ahead of the range. As the entire available space was only about seven feet by eight feet, every inch was precious. Food, clothes and bedding had to be stored, too, the latter usually in drawers under the cross-bed. Food was kept outside in a cupboard in the butty's stern where it could be kept cool. So, at night the boatman and his wife would sleep in the cross-bed, the two youngest children on the side-beds, two older children in the fore-cabin, and any other older children on the side-bed of the after-cabin of the other boat.

As I have said, the butty was always considered to be the wife's boat. She kept the cabin clean and lived in this boat, and it was always the butty boat was prettied up with polished brass and lace plates. The leading boat was the husband's and he was responsible for its upkeep and cleaning and of course, in the later days of steam and diesel, for looking after the engine.

This life, with the whole family continually on the move, meant that the children could get no formal education, even after the Education Act of 1870. They were rarely in any one place long enough to be able to attend a school. Consequently, several generations of boat people were completely illiterate. But the children were under their father's eye the whole time - unlike the children of factory or farm workers, whose fathers were away each day for long hours. So the boat people developed a completely patriarchal system. The children quite naturally from their earliest days picked up the canal skills, so they were trained - or rather, gradually picked up how - to steer a narrow boat from the age of about eight upwards. A boy of eight could easily steer a motor boat pulling a butty and do it very efficiently He could be absolutely first-rate at doing the job. There were no kinds of legal restrictions either at this time. The children would also be quite capable of getting the locks ready. Those children might not have been able to read and write but they were probably a great deal better educated in the true sense than many who could. They had acquired a body of useful skills, together with what in today's jargon would be called a "work ethic" and they were contented.

But the do-gooders cannot be content with the fact that people are different. Everyone must be the same, according to them. So in about 1950, Birmingham City Council opened a hostel for canal children in the Birmingham area at Wood End, Erdington, which took about 16 children. It was not a success. The children would be left at the hostel for about three months, like a boarding school. In theory the parents could visit them whenever they were in the area, but in practice the parents were only in the Birmingham area very rarely and, when they were, there was always a great deal to be done, discharging, loading, and all the paper work with the clerks. Then there were fares to be paid for, out of very meagre wages, to get to and from the hostel. The result was that they did not see their children anything like as much as was desirable. These children were aged between about 12 and 14, so they were already fully into the way of life on boats. They could see no real purpose in the schooling they were getting, they felt resentful and were very unhappy because they wanted to be on the boats with their parents. By the time term was over the children were virtually out of control. They would come home for the holidays and their parents just could not do anything with them. This was one of the principal reasons for the break-up of the family boat.

Another reason for the break-up of the traditional family boat system, in my opinion, was occasioned by the denationalisation of road transport by the government, which I mention in a later chapter. The loss of work this caused meant that many families whose forebears had worked the canals for generations could no longer afford to do so. They found other, more lucrative work, away from the canals. They went to work on building sites and, ironically enough, in later years, many of them found employment building motorways.

Of the few people working the canals now, most are not members of long-established boater families, but young people who have become fed up with the rat-race of our large urban centres, and have taken up the life because they want to get away from it all. In a sense, I suppose, I also started as a boatman in order to get away from it all. But there was still much to do before I could actually begin to work. The first thing was to get a crew. I was not married in those days so had no worry about accommodating a family. During a discussion with the previous owners to see what I could do about crews, they said "We know a boatman, Tom Jackson, who has a teenage son, and we are sure he would be prepared to come and work for you. But it would be better if you had three to a crew."

So when I bought the boats I talked to Tom Jackson, who worked as a boatman for the Grand Union Canal Carrying Company, and whose family had been working boatmen for several generations. We had further discussions about the details of running a pair of boats, and also the question of manning. Tom's son, Jim, was then 19 and had been working for his father. At that time Jim was actually with his father's boat, tied up at Hawkesbury Stop near Coventry, or 'Sutton's' as the boatmen called it. In spite of his youth, Jim was a very experienced boatman. His father agreed that he should come to work for me, virtually as my captain, that is, responsible for the maintenance and running of my boats and their equipment, subject of course, to my own approval and supervision as owner.

The third member of the crew was a chap called Eric Hill, who preferred to be known as Joe. Whilst on LSTs (Landing Ship Tanks) during the war, Joe, on duty on the bridge, got talking to me. He was then a lad of about 18. It seemed that he was rather lost at home and was not very happy in his job. He mentioned that he had no prospect once the war was over and had no idea what he was going to do. He seemed to me a very sensible, likeable sort, and I said that if I was ever in a position to offer him a job, I would do so. So, two years after the war ended, I thought of him, rummaged around, found his address and wrote to him. I have no idea what he had been doing in the meantime, but whatever it was he said he was interested in my offer. I arranged to meet him in a pub in Hale (Cheshire) one week-end, and there I explained my plans to him. He was tickled pink with the idea of working on the canals, so I "signed him on", as it were, verbally, then and there.

I had, of course, explored the possibility of likely business on the canals, and had undertaken to do sub-contract work for the Grand Union Canal Carrying Company. There was plenty of work, and the Company was very happy about my arrangements. The late owners, H. Dean and Sons moved out, and I moved from my comfortable suburban home at Wimbledon into a pair of canal boats at Bulls Bridge, Southall. What a completely different existence it was; something like serving in drifters, on which I had been at the beginning of the war, but the atmosphere was so completely different from anything I had encountered before. Everybody was so very friendly and so willing to help; from the boat manager at Bulls Bridge, Mr Wood, to all the boatmen that I met. Jim now moved into the after cabin on *Columba*, and he made the new rope fenders we needed and set to on other jobs such as replacing the ropes and checking equipment.

Amongst these jobs were checking the shafts and making mops for cleaning the boats. Each boat had two shafts, used for pushing off from the banks or in shallows. One of these, usually about 20 feet long, stays on the beams and is traditionally painted in a single colour, usually the main colour of the boat and in this case dark grey. The second, the cabin shaft, is about six feet long and is painted in traditional primary colours in short sections all along its length. This is kept close to hand on the cabin roof.

Mops were made from old overcoats, and were far superior to anything you could buy. Strips of cloth about two inches wide and some two feet long were cut from the material. These were arranged criss-cross like a multi-pointed star, and were fixed to the end of the mop pole using a square-sectioned brad or nail, with a washer to keep the bits of cloth in place, hammered into a hole drilled into the pole so that the wood would not split. It was necessary to use a square nail so that when the mop was being twirled, as it was constantly when in use for drying, the cloth would not revolve.

The set-up was this. In the motor boat I had the new cabin, and Jim occupied the other one (which is traditionally the captain's on a canal boat). Joe was to have the cabin in the butty *Uranus* where we would also eat, have our radio and spend much of our spare time, such as it was. I had a car. and to save expense I arranged with Joe that he should travel to Wolverhampton by train and I would pick him up there and take him to Bulls Bridge.

Having loaded with fuel, all was now ready for our first carrying job. We went to Brentford, about four miles from Bulls Bridge. On that first short trip as a professional boatman, I passed over that triple bridge that I had first seen in the illustration in *Transport and Travel Monthly,* way back in 1918. We loaded with about 50 tons of maize which was to be taken to a firm in Fenny Stratford. This was a trip of about 55 miles, with some 73 locks to negotiate. It was important that the load should be evenly distributed so that the boats sat correctly in the water. As the propeller tended to pull down the stern of the motor boat, it was best to load so *Columba* was slightly down by the bows, then when under way she would be swimming level.

Having discharged our cargo, we went on empty to the Coventry coalfields where at Newdigate Colliery we took on a consignment of coal for John Dickinson's Mill at Croxley, where the well-known Basildon Bond writing paper was made. This presented us with a practical experience which luckily posed no problem for us, thanks to Jim. *Columba,* as I have mentioned, had an extended after-cabin that had been added by the Deans, which was very convenient when working three-handed. This extra cabin, however, meant that if loaded in the normal way, *Columba* would be bows heavy, so we should be riding with the stern further out of the water than it should be. To correct this, we used slack boards for the last 12 feet before the cabin. With these boards, each about five or six feet long and two feet high, more coal could be stacked at this point (an additional 8 to 12 tons) thus levelling us off again. Motor and butty together held something up to 53 tons (depending on the type and size of coal) and on both boats this amount of cargo would give us a freeboard of about six inches. Because of this, side cloths would be used, but not top cloths, unless our loading instructions (written or verbal) specified that the boats had to be fully sheeted up - as might happen in wet weather, for instance, or with certain cargoes that could be affected by damp.

This coal trip from Coventry to Croxley became quite a frequent one for us. Sometimes we collected from Measham Colliery at the head of the Ashby Canal, or from Pooley Hall Colliery at Polesworth, but Newdigate was always the easiest one for us. This was because at Newdigate the railway lines ran alongside the canal, so the wagons were parallel to and quite near the boats. All that was required was to put a wooden chute across the gap and we could shovel the coal straight in with no fuss, just moving the boats along from time to time to ensure even distribution of the load.

Other loads that we often took northwards from Brentford or Regents Canal Dock were timber and sugar. We also carried loose grain, mostly wheat or maize, generally delivering this either at Northampton or Fenny Stratford. A quite frequent pattern we adopted was to go from London to Northampton loaded, then empty to the Coventry coalfields, load with coal and back to London.

It was on our first trip that we came across a rather strange craft. We were just coming up to Rickmansworth Lock when we spotted a paddle boat. Pleasure boats, unlike today, were not very common on the canals. This was a converted army pontoon, and was owned by the architect, Eric de Maré and his wife. They were working their way up the Grand Union Canal taking photographs and making drawings. Eric de Maré was later to write a whole special supplement for the *Architectural Review* dealing with the architecture of the canals, the painting and design of the boats, the ironwork and everything seen on the canals. When we came into the lock, Mr de Maré took photographs of *Columba* and *Uranus*.

At Fenny Stratford, too, we made our first acquaintance with the landlord of the Red Lion pub. It was a tatty little pub, and its bar looked more like the waiting room of a railway station than a pub. But the usefulness of the Red Lion lay in this very untidiness, for it was created by crates and boxes of provisions spread all over the place. It was a very handy provisioning place. Working canals were strange to me, and with not much help in the way of guides, I was only too grateful for any helpful advice from people who knew the ropes. One friend, Mr Finch, who was actually the insurance underwriter that dealt with my insurance and who lived at Boxmoor, wrote out these notes to help me on my first few trips.

Rickmansworth Suburban canal precincts have their own atmosphere.

Watford Good shopping place if you can get into the town.

Columba and *Uranus* below Maffers (Marsworth) in 1951, with Wally steering. Alf Best about to get off at bridge 'ole with bike.

Boxmoor at Fishery Inn Alongside last lock north, you'd probably be able to wangle a bath if you 'work into' the atmosphere of the proprietor. . .

Tring Station Large hotel about 200 yards east (There's no lock here - it's on Summit level) – not brilliant but might be useful.

Marsworth & Wilstone Reservoirs Cut runs alongside. Bleak - much bird-life if you're interested. Then flattish rough pasture country. I believe there's a good pub here but I haven't explored it.

Slapton Lock 400 yards east is a thatched pub - I think it's the *Carpenters Arms*, rough but hearty. Then another 4 miles flat pastures along the canal.

Leighton Buzzard Many boats tie up here - particularly at weekends. In town, ½ mile east is a fairly decent cafe on south side of market place before you get to Town Hall. Good for a meal. After Leighton Lock you come to:

Jackdaw Pound Believe rather a tricky stretch. 1½ miles north of Leighton Lock is a farm on a hill on west side of cut by a bridge carrying a field track. Owned by Hopkins - *Broad Oaks*. He ought to be good for a pint of milk sometimes.

Three Locks New Inn on west side of northern-most lock – Aylesbury Brewery Co. - beer not over well-kept. Mrs Hammond, very respectable widow in command. Prompt closing! You can buy confectionery here on usual points! I've seen boats tie up here. It's quiet but cheery in pub sometimes on Saturday night. At next bridge north the village bathes, not so bad, but muddy after boats pass.

Fenny Stratford Good for shopping in Bletchley. Then you have 9 miles with no locks of very quiet undulating pastures up to:

Wolverton A lousy place with a filthy mile alongside LMS Railway Carriage Works, then across an aqueduct over River Ouse (the Pig Trough), another mile to:

Cosgrove Then another 5 miles very quiet up to:

Stoke Bruerne Several locks. There used to be a very good all-round shop here and a nurse in a cottage alongside the northern-most lock if you want any medical treatment.

Very few boats seem to run on Sunday morning. I think all the boatmen have a lie in!

Much of this information is concerned with shopping and food, a highly important aspect of daily life. As the mention of "points" will remind us, many foodstuffs and sweets were still rationed. To know of places where you could get a good meal (one did not have to produce a ration book for meals eaten in a restaurant) was a most useful way of helping out the rations. Also, for a three-man crew with limited cooking facilities, it had another great attraction - less cooking!

On board, the cooking was shared between the members of the crew, and, of course, the menu depended a great deal upon who was cook for that particular meal. My speciality was a fish pie made of tinned pilchards and potatoes. Another dish I did regularly was smoked haddock cooked with onions in milk, and served with mashed potatoes. Bacon and eggs and baked beans also played a large part in the general diet, all washed down with innumerable cups of tea - not served from a Measham teapot; these were always kept for show, even in traditional families, and only came out on special occasions like weddings, christenings and funerals.

Chapter Two

WORKING THE CANALS

Once having settled down to the job, things went reasonably smoothly. But not everything on the canals was rosy. One bane that came to light early on was the question of pollution. Just after we had discharged our cargo at Dickinson's Mill, Croxley, we had to go through Croxley Lock. Here we discovered that because of the acids being discharged into the waters of the canal the lock was covered in foam about two feet deep. What is more, this foam made everything it touched extremely slippery. You can imagine the danger this would be to boat families. Many had small children on board and it would have been all too easy for a child to slip off the bows and fall in without anyone being aware of it. After this first experience of the danger and talking about it, and hearing the stories about it told by other boatmen, I sat down and wrote to the Inland Waterways Association and complained and suggested that some action should be taken.

I had a letter back from the Chairman and Co-Founder of the Association, Robert Aickman, thanking me for pointing out the danger and inviting me to call in and see him the next time the boats were in London. This I promptly did and as a result I was asked to join the Council of the IWA. Other Council members at this time included the Earl of Lucan (father of the Earl who disappeared), a most charming man who represented Labour in the House of Lords; Tom Rolt, the author, and his wife Angela; Charles Hadfield, the author and publisher; Sonia Smith, who will be mentioned again later on, and Elizabeth Jane Howard, the novelist.

Nowadays, for pleasure boating on the canals, the usual way of calculating the time for a journey depends on two things - the maximum speed allowed of four miles an hour and the fact that holidaying crews often take 15 minutes to work through a lock although many do less. So, as both travelling one mile and going through one lock each take a quarter of an hour, adding together the number of miles and the number of locks and dividing the sum by four gives you the approximate time taken in hours e.g. 26 miles and 40 locks:

$$26 + 40 = 66$$

$$66 \div 4 = 16\tfrac{1}{2} \text{ hours}$$

However, as working boatmen, we could reckon to be faster moving than this. When you know what you are doing, it is possible to cut down the time taken to work a lock to five minutes. The difference between four locks an hour and twelve an hour obviously means greater speed for a journey. So that the journey mentioned in the previous chapter, Brentford to Fenny Stratford, with 73 locks in 55 miles would take us about 21 hours altogether.

The timing for one of our round trips would be something like this. First, loading at Brentford with grain would take about three or four hours, followed by 21 hours to get to Fenny Stratford and another three or four hours to unload. Travelling empty to Newdigate would account for some further 22 hours, with another four for loading. Back to

London would take about 43 hours, and unloading another four. This makes up a total of some 102 working hours. As we were usually up at six or just after, and ready to start a day's work by seven at the latest, and knocked off at about seven each evening, this work-load would be spread over about eight or nine days.

Of course, when approaching locks, you never knew whether they were going to be "for" you or "against" you, or whether another pair of boats was approaching from the opposite direction. To eliminate arguments about priority over locks, each had two distance posts, one above and one below the lock, and the procedure was normally that whoever passed one of these distance posts first had priority through the lock. In the interests of economy of water however, it was general practice that a boat working down to a full lock or one working up to an empty lock went through first, providing it was within half a mile of the lock. I must say that, as with most things on the canals, the boatmen have a great sense of camaraderie, and everything was done with a good spirit. There was the occasional stroppy boatman who preferred to be unpleasant, but they were few and far between.

Journey time could also be cut down where there was a lock-keeper who could prepare the locks in readiness for your arrival and this could sometimes be ensured by telephoning ahead. At this time, about fifty per cent of the locks had their own lock-keepers to look after them.

Our first real snag turned up whilst cleaning the boats after unloading a cargo. To do this, the bottom boards should be lifted to give access to the elm planks of the actual structure of the boat. Whilst owned by Dean's, this had apparently been done rarely or not at all, and because of the lack of experience of narrow boats on the part of the surveyor, they were not taken up for the survey. It was on the first occasion that Jim lifted the boards that he spotted some rot in the elm planks.

If wet elm is not dried out properly, it goes sappy, a form of rot which seemed to have developed on *Columba* and to a lesser extent on *Uranus* during a period just before the war. During this bad spell for canals the two boats had been laid up - none too efficiently, it would seem - and the rot had gone unnoticed ever since. It seemed to me to be rather dangerous, as there was a large number of pits in the wood, some as big as saucers, and between one and two inches deep. I got an opinion on the situation at Bulls Bridge; they said we ought to take the boats out of service and have them repaired.

Unfortunately, Bulls Bridge Boatyard was so busy with its own repairs that they could not fit us in, so I had to look round for somewhere else. I chased around and found a yard in Birmingham called Spencer Abbott, who would do the job reasonably cheaply as well. *Columba* needed about thirteen of her elm planks replacing, and *Uranus* about seven. Most of the damage appeared to have occurred at the place where the metal sides were bolted to the wood at the knee bolts, which made the job a bit trickier to carry out. Although this was the only work which was essential, I decided that whilst the boats were laid up, I would have the engines overhauled and the boats repainted.

When I took them over they were painted very simply in dark grey, and lined red, with the legend "H Dean & Son" on the side in white with orange shading, and they looked rather dull. Spencer Abbott seemed to have some good ideas on painting and they were also agents for a good brand of paint made by

Columba at the Spencer, Abbot yard on the Birmingham & Fazeley Canal near Salford Junction.

Mason's of Derby.

I went through Mason's colour book, and there found a red which was really the most brilliant I have ever seen. It was called "Ayres Coach Red" and it was basically red with an orange tint to it. We had the boats painted in this colour, with green lining; the cabin tops were done in maroon. The butty was done up to look like a wedding cake and they were both very beautiful.

Top sheets were used to cover the cargo and they usually had just the firm's name lettered on them. We had ours re-tarred to protect them and on them we had written in white the words "Use Inland Waterways" in letters about a foot high. It was really a most effective advertising medium.

There seems to be a misconception about the painting of narrow boats. Many people appear to think that the boatmen used to paint them themselves, but the painting was as specialised a job as their actual building. The boatmen would take their boats to a specialist boat-painter when they needed refurbishing and most of the painters were employed by the boatyards.

Fellows, Morton and Clayton had a painter at their yard at Uxbridge. Walkers of Rickmansworth used to paint. L. B. Faulkner of Leighton Buzzard had an excellent painter called Frank Jones. Bushells of Tring and Samuel Barlow at Braunston both employed painters. Another famous painter was at Braunston too; Frank Nurser was the painter at the yard originally owned by the Nurser Brothers.

The actual patterns used on the boats probably came from the gypsy tradition, although any boatman would strongly deny that he was a gypsy or that any of his family ever were. There is, however, a strong family likeness between the traditional designs on gypsy caravans and those used on narrow boats. Each of the painters had the same repertoire of designs - castles, roses and geometrical shapes, especially circles and diamonds - but each had his own distinctive style. All the roses painted by Frank Nurser were the same, for instance, and the roses painted by Frank Jones at Leighton Buzzard were all the same, but there were subtle nuances. To people who were not of the canals they all looked alike, but boatmen could tell which boats had been done by which painter, just by looking at them.

The traditional treatment was to have roses and castles painted on the doors into the cabin and engine room, and on the rear panel on each side of the butty boat. Geometrical pattern went on the tiller, the gunwales of bow and stern, and the triangular top of the bow. These geometrical patterns consisted mostly of squares, circles and borders. Roses were also used to decorate such things as the water cans and hand bowls used on board the narrow boats.

The Docks and Inland Waterways Executive (D & IWE), as they were then called, caused some consternation among boatmen not long after nationalisation when they announced their scheme for the repainting of the new nationally-owned fleet of narrow boats. They were going to paint the cabin panels plain yellow, with a narrow blue line around them, and 'British Waterways' painted in blue on the cabin sides. No roses, no castles, no geometrical patterns - all traditions gone in one fell swoop - and the predominant colours for the new scheme yellow and blue, ones which had never ever been used for the all-over painting of boats before. The outcry was backed up by the Inland Waterways Association, who at that time had very little influence compared with what they have today. One of the chief protagonists in this was a girl called Sonia South, who had married a boatman called George Smith. She was outside the thing, so she could do it with a detached view, because she worked, not for British Waterways, but for the Samuel Barlow Coal Company, which always gave its boats the full treatment - one of their boats appears on the front cover of Tom Rolt's book *The Inland Waterways of England*. So Sonia Smith lobbied everyone, but she barely raised a spark of interest. Not even the Trades Union showed any interest; they probably did not understand, and if they did understand, they just did not care. In the end, the Docks and Inland Waterways Executive had their way, and the canal scene became the poorer visually as a result.

Chapter Three

THE KENNET & AVON CANAL

During the six weeks or so that the *Columba* and *Uranus* were going to be laid up for repairs, the three of us could have a holiday. I decided to make mine a busman's holiday and, with a friend from Wolverhampton, to explore the length of the Kennet and Avon Canal. We agreed that the simplest method of exploration was by bicycle, for we knew the canal suffered from neglect and was not passable by boat in many places.

I had previously heard of a trip by narrow boat *Westminster* which was owned by William Bennett, with Gerry Bird as his crew. They set off from Avonmouth, and got through to Hovis at Newbury. This was quite an achievement as *Westminster* was the first boat with a cargo to go through from west to east for a number of years, and indeed she was the last working boat to do so. Their cargo was ten tons of flour for Hovis. They had a terrible time getting through, and had to be pulled by horses, tractors and gangs of men, but they were able to complete the journey in spite of all the obstacles put in their way by the owners, the Great Western Railway or British Railways as they were to become. It might perhaps be said that it was fortunate that William Bennett was a solicitor and knew all the answers. Since that trip, I knew conditions must have deteriorated and I wanted to find out just how much.

The Kennet and Avon Canal was opened in 1810, having cost some £900,000 to build. It survived as an independent canal until 1854 when it was bought by the Great Western Railway. During its most profitable years, 1830 to 1850, it used to transport annually about 340,000 tons of assorted freights, from coal to building stone. The time from London Bridge to Bath was reduced from up to four weeks by horse drawn wagon to between four and six days, with an extra day to Bristol, and the weight of an unsplit load was increased from about six tons to upwards of ninety tons in a wide boat.

As might be expected, the Great Western Railway was hardly interested in promoting and maintaining a rival to its own railway transport interests, so the Kennet and Avon Canal was allowed to drift into disuse and dereliction. It is an old policy - you make something difficult to use, then claim correctly that it is not being used sufficiently to keep it going and close it down. British Railways used exactly the same policy on the Bristol to Chipping Sodbury Railway line. Here was a rapidly growing "dormitory" area with hundreds of its residents working in Bristol who would have been quite happy to travel in each day by train. The first train in the morning arrived at Temple Meads at about five past nine, and the last train in the evening left at ten minutes to five. The nine-to-five office workers could not use the trains; the line was declared uneconomic and passenger trains ceased to run. A change of time by about half an hour would have made all the difference, but no, official policy was all against it, as it was with the Kennet and Avon Canal. This is only a small example; hundreds of miles of similar branch and even main lines were closed in the same manner.

On my trip along the canal from Bath I kept short notes of the state of the canal, its locks, bridges and so forth, and also of the canal-side pubs and shops. Time and again the entries show that the swing bridges across the canal were locked into position so that they could not be opened to let boats through. There was also a great deal of damage. From Lock 22 to Lock 38 there were no fewer than 13 broken balance beams, and two sets of gates were in a very bad state of repair. Another note that occurs with monotonous regularity is "weed very bad" and in several sections, just beyond Bradford-on-Avon, for example, and at Semington, there is a note indicating that the reeds were growing across the complete width of the canal.

Another note indicates wilful obstruction of the canal during the war. Apparently top army brass, for some reason, decided that the route of the Kennet and Avon Canal would become an important defensive line across the country in case of invasion. To this end, numerous pill-boxes and tank-traps in the form of huge concrete truncated pyramids were erected along the length of the navigation. But at Devizes I noted the most ridiculous piece of military reasoning: "Tank barriers on inside of cut in bed 200 yards west of Horton Bridge". Did the big-wigs envisage the enemy tanks (presumably parachuted in) travelling up the bed of the canal?

From Lock 65, I began to measure the depth of the water at places where measurements could be conveniently taken. The stretch from here to Lock 83, where we finished our journey, seemed to be mostly between four and six feet deep, but there were places where it was much shallower than that; two feet nine inches at Lock 73, for instance, and two feet six at Lock 67. However, on the whole we were heartened by the general condition of the canal. All the locks at Devizes seemed to be in a reasonable working order, even if many balance beams did need renewing. There were other encouraging signs at Melksham where an empty pound was discovered to be caused by two locks above the junction being repaired, and there were also now foot walks on some of the lock gates.

Also encouraging was the fact that near Bradford-on-Avon there was someone who was interested in using the canal for pleasure boating, an interesting foretaste of what was to follow later. A further indication of a difficulty in trying to reopen the canals of England is shown in a note I made at Seend. It reads, "Obstructive tenant to cottages who takes the view that the lock is private property. Lock No. 22." Need it be pointed out that this is in spite of the canals being nationally owned at this time!

It did seem to me however, that it would not be possible to get narrow boats to work through the canal with the same techniques as those used on the Grand Union Canal. There were three main reasons for this conclusion. The first was because the paddle gear was so difficult to use. The normal Grand Union paddle gear was very efficient and easy to use: even the new Hatton Locks, with their infamous form of paddle gear, were child's play compared with those on the Kennet and Avon.

The second difficulty was presented by the Kennet and Avon locks, many of which were boarded up to water level and turf-sided above that. Because of this, they lacked any stumps or checking posts for boats using downhill runners or uphill straps. It meant that if you wanted to use the locks with a pair of boats then you would have to breast up the boats below every lock, which of course is a shocking waste of time and would double or treble the time taken to work through the locks.

The third thing we noticed was the lack of ground paddles. On the Grand Union Canal, both the top and bottom gates have four paddles and there are ground paddles as well. These latter are operated first to let the water in under the boats and to lift them up; when the water has come up to a certain point, the gate paddles are then opened. Because the water is coming in under the boats instead of being forced down from the gates across the cill onto the boats, there is less chance of damage to the boats working up through the locks. The extra paddles, of course, also help to fill and empty the locks more rapidly, thus cutting down valuable time on a journey. A further point we noticed was that there were no jumping-off points above the locks or steps down from the locks.

We eventually got to Newbury, where I called on John Gould, one of the most stalwart proponents for the reopening of the Kennet and Avon. I went to see him because I wanted to tell him about the journey that I had just made along the canal as far as Newbury from Bath, and also (with my new born enthusiasm) to see whether it was possible to get some trade onto the canal, probably from the eastern end, which seemed to be the most feasible in view of its proximity to the canals leading up to the Midlands. I met, through John Gould, the Chairman of the local branch of the Inland Waterways Association. John Lester was also the Managing Director of the Newbury Laundry. He told me they used large quantities of salt in the laundering process, so with the Cerebos agent from whom they got their salt, we had a discussion to see what could be done to get the salt to Newbury from the Cerebos factory at Middlewich, very conveniently situated alongside the canal.

Unfortunately, at that time it was not possible to get a reasonable through toll from the Potteries down to Oxford and from Reading to Newbury, so everything rather fell into abeyance, but we all kept our options open to see what we could do later on.

Chapter Four

CHANGES

It was in June 1949 that Joe decided to leave. I did not see him again. I think he left England and went out east, to what used to be the Anglo-Iranian Oil Company. We were now two-handed, although from time to time we had the occasional help for a week at a stretch of a young man called Fred Hobbs. He was a useful stop-gap, but did not seem interested in becoming a full-time boatman. For our first trip after Joe's departure, we went down to Brentford to load. This was to be a memorable event. I had previously made arrangements with a photographer in Brentford to come and take pictures of the boats after docking at Spencer Abbott. We loaded for Tyseley Wharf in Birmingham with a cargo of spelter. It is probably hard to believe in these days of lower maintenance, but we had 53 tons on, 30 tons in the butty *Uranus* and 23 in *Columba*.

This was an ideal cargo, as *Columba* was unaffected by the reduced hold size caused by her long cabin. Her capacity was about average for a small Woolwich when we were using slack boards, even with coal or grain, although these cargoes did involve more work with trimming. So we were loaded and clothed up by mid-morning and ready for Jack Gashion, who took some beautiful photographs of the boats as a pair and also of *Columba* by herself with Jim at the tiller. And then my mother came to see us and made us a wonderful stew. We moved off in the late afternoon for Bulls Bridge, where we spent the night ready for an early start next morning and the assault on the 140 locks and 125 miles and 4 furlongs to Birmingham. In spite of being now two-handed, we were to cover this in 52½ hours, even with our load of 53 tons. This gave an average speed of 2.4 miles an hour. If I remember rightly, we had a very good road and decent weather.

After this run, I recall that we had a series of good runs with quick cargoes and then we decided during a slack period to have a change. We left the butty behind and set off for Ellesmere Port via the Birmingham Canals and Wolverhampton Locks. All the locks north of Birmingham were single, which was why we did not take *Uranus* with us. So through Birmingham and down Wolverhampton 21 to Aldersley Junction we went, going on the Staffordshire and Worcestershire Canal. Half a mile further on we made a sharp turn to the left on to the practically dead straight of the "Shroppie", or to give it its full former title, the "Shropshire Union Section of the London, Midland and Scottish Railway Company's Canals". Telford's Birmingham and Liverpool Junction Canal, which was to become part of the Shropshire Union Canal, was taken over by the London North Western Railway under an arrangement which would guarantee them an annual dividend, which meant that the Shropshire Union was independent from the LNW.

The Shropshire Union Canal system is the very large and extensive layout of canals originally designed by Thomas Telford to serve the Ellesmere district and North Wales. It covers the area between the River Mersey and Newtown in Montgomeryshire (now

Powys), through Ellesmere Port on the south bank of the River Mersey. In all there are approximately 200 miles of canal with 127 locks, surely an indication of Telford's genius as an engineer when the nature of the countryside is considered. *[Note: Telford designed only parts of the SU system.]* Compare this with the 140 locks for 125 miles of the Grand Union and 92 locks for 33 miles of the Rochdale Canal. Obviously, you cannot equate mileage with locks but it was evidence of Telford's genius, assisted no doubt by developments in surveying equipment and additional money that was available, that he was able to get the most out of his skills and produce a modern, labour-saving canal. This is also shown on the Macclesfield Canal, where he was able to concentrate all the trade on only two long levels linked by a flight of comparatively easily-worked locks.

You may well think that I am somewhat biased in my remarks about the Shropshire Union. Having read Tom Rolt's description of it in *Narrow Boat*, this may well be so. Mr Rolt says:

> "Construction of the Birmingham and Liverpool Junction Canal was not commenced until 1826, and so far as I know, it was the last important waterway, excluding ship canals, to be built in this country. Its inception was entirely due to the success of George Stephenson's Liverpool and Manchester Railway, for the canal proprietor, alarmed by the threat of their new competitor, desired a quicker and easier route between the two great industrial areas. For this reason it is unequalled by any waterway in the magnitude of its earthworks and the directness of its course. Across the land pastures from Nantwich, through Hack Green to Audlem, it cuts as straight as a Roman road, and for the first and only time in our travels we found ourselves wishing that *Cressy* was capable of a little more speed. The older, winding waterways fully gratified that chief joy of travel, the expectation of what may be round the next corner, but here, when our attention had been focused on abridge, perhaps a mile distant, this element was entirely lacking and our progress seemed intolerably slow."

So we turned left at Autherley Junction on to the Shroppie, passing under the bridge which carries the Staffordshire and Worcestershire towpath and through the stop lock, to receive a cheery greeting from the toll clerk, Sam Lomas. I was now beginning to realise (if I had not already done so) how very useful was *Bradshaw's Canals and Navigable Rivers of England and Wales* by Henry Rodolf de Salis, Assoc.M.Inst.C.E. and a former Chairman of Fellows, Morton and Clayton Ltd, Canal Carriers. It has proved a most useful source of information on canals. I write nearly 50 years on from that purchase from Napier's second-hand book and furniture shop in Walpole Road, Wimbledon, and the actual copy of the 1928 edition still rests on my desk as I write. Besides being grateful for Bradshaw's handbook, I also bless the day when I decided to buy copies of the one-inch Ordnance Survey maps of all the canals I travelled, as these, too, proved invaluable.

Sam advised us that there was a good shop and Post Office at Wheaton Aston, so we cast off and set course for there. We discovered that the Shroppie was rather a shallow canal for even a small Woolwich, so we had to proceed at about three-quarters of our normal speed to keep her off the bottom. Even so, we were able to maintain three miles an hour without too much difficulty. We arrived at Wheaton Aston bridge, tied up near the bridge hole and I set out on the bike for the shop. This was run by a most charming lady who was also the Post-Mistress. On my return we went through the lock on to the 13½ mile pound to Tyrley Top Lock. The scenery was quite spectacular and equalled only by Telford's massive engineering works, a truly wonderful achievement when it is realised that there was no mechanical equipment, not even early steam shovels, and that everything was achieved by men, women and children with shovels and baskets, gunpowder, and literally hundreds of horses. Anybody who saw the early parts of the serial *God's Wonderful Railway*, shown on BBC1, will know what I mean.

When we got to Norbury Junction, we were given a friendly wave by some of the staff there, one of whom I had already met and got to know better years later when I went to live on the Kennet and Avon Canal at Bathampton. He was George Lloyd, the future Divisional Engineer for the South West. There are points of interest all the way up the Shroppie; the junction at Norbury, now disused, leading down to the Shrewsbury canals; the staggeringly deep cuttings with their lofty over-bridges; the depths of Tyrley cutting where I saw my first fire-flies; Adderley Locks (five); the flight at Audlem followed by the two locks at Hack Green; Hurleston Junction with the arm to the Ellesmere Canals and the canal to Newtown (soon to be reopened, it is hoped); the canal to Llangollen, and of course the Pontcysyllte and Chirk Aqueducts. Then there was Barbridge Junction with the branch to Middlewich, which we were to travel on a later occasion. A feature worth noting about this junction was the two covered loading bays, since demolished, across the arm rather in the nature of one of Brunel's over-all roof stations, such as in early days at Didcot or Bath.

Next of interest is the iron lock - I think below Beeston Castle - iron because it was built on quicksand, and then finally into Chester with three formidably deep locks in a flight. You come out of the bottom lock under a low railway bridge with a sharp right turn. It was all fun in the days of steam, when we would see the express from Paddington to Birkenhead with its phenomenally long destination boards, which I seem to remember included Paddington, Birmingham (Snow Hill), Wolverhampton (Low Level), Shrewsbury, Gobowen, Ruabon, Chester and Birkenhead.

And so on to Ellesmere Port, the centre designed by Telford as the magnet for Ellesmere and its trade. It had magnificent basins and extensive and handsome warehouses, some alas to be destroyed by fire in 1970. But Telford's dream did not fully materialise, for the Ellesmere system of canals was never completed. Later the canals were taken over by the London and North Western Railway. In 1937 the arm to Newtown was breached and in spite of the requirements of the Act when it was purchased, the LMS did not repair the break, leaving a single boat trading on the isolated branch. Then in 1945 the Railway, by Act of Parliament, closed the branch and certain other waterways, such as the Huddersfield Narrow Canal and Standedge Tunnel, the longest and highest in the country. It is wonderful what you can get away with when people's minds are preoccupied with more important things.

There seemed to be the same trend as down south with regards to cargo, because we were told that we would be loading flour for Stourport, but not for two days, so we decided to regard the interim as a holiday. Jim and I went off to see the sights of Liverpool. I cannot remember exactly how we got there, or what we did when we arrived. We did, I know, spend one evening on the overhead Railway, since demolished. It was an interesting experience and reminded me of the subway in New York, on which I had travelled when I was there in 1943. Both were in some respect like the raised sections of the London Underground. In 1943 the New York subway was pretty clean, although not as clean as the London Underground, even in wartime. I often wonder what Americans must think when they come over to London today and compare our comparatively spotless, largely graffiti-free stations and coaches with the sordid state of theirs.

Anyhow, back to Ellesmere and loading. We put on board 20 tons of bagged flour in two hundredweight sacks for the River Severn Warehouse at Stourport. Now that we had our cargo, our main aim was to get rid of it as quickly as possible, so no hanging about, as we had wasted enough time already. We made good time to Autherley Junction where we received instructions from our friend Sam Lomas, the toll clerk, to ring up when we got to Compton on the Staffordshire and Worcestershire Canal if we were having any trouble with our load. I do not think they had seen anything so large as a small Woolwich before — it was a good thing we were not a big Woolwich. We had trouble almost directly we had passed Aldersley Junction, where the Birmingham Canals come in, the way from which we had come. In spite of difficulty, we staggered on to Compton, on the bottom or in liquid mud most of the way. We were told, "Carry on as best you can. Help will come tomorrow." Imagine our joy and surprise when, arriving at Wightwick Lock, we were greeted by two chaps and a large, grey horse. They were instructed to come with us as far as Kidderminster, towing us through the bad spots. Naturally, Jim and I became very good friends with all three of our new mates.

Loading 2cwt bags of flour

Every fresh canal has features of interest peculiar to itself. We were to come across many on the Staffordshire and Worcestershire southern half. The northern half (of which more anon) runs from Autherley Junction to Great Haywood Junction, and is shorter by two miles with only 11 locks as against 31 for the southern half. So we were for it. Thirty-one locks in 25 miles, some of them most unusual; however, we were now four-handed and had a horse! It is sad, but although I took a photograph of the chaps, I cannot remember their names, or that of the horse, but they

Jim (left) and our three friends on the Stafford & Worcester in 1949.

were, I know, very cheerful and willing, one in his fifties and the other early thirties. I think they thought it all a bit of a lark, particularly as the weather was so fine.

The first of the unusual locks was at the Bratch. All three locks had top and bottom gates, but the pounds between the middle one and the outer two were only about 15 feet long, so although they were separate, they could just a easily have been built as a staircase lock. They were followed almost immediately by Bumble Hole Bridge and lock, a strange-sounding name, but no more so than Cowroast. Then one more lock and Botterham staircase and then right in the middle of a spinney and some ploughed fields, Swindon Iron Works. It was here that we saw coming towards us, on a canal in Great Western Railway territory, a very elegant horse-boat in the black and white livery of the London, Midland and Scottish Railway. I cannot be sure of her name, but I think it was the *Antwerp*. Clearly, this required looking into. Fortunately our horsey friends were able to supply the explanation. The southern half of the Staffordshire and Worcestershire was in Great Western territory; the LMS had no lines in the area, so to get traffic they ran these ex-Shroppie fly boats. For many years, they had cornered virtually the whole of the carpet trade from Kidderminster which went, I believe, to their warehouses and wharves at Tipton, and there was really nothing the GWR could do about it, as they did not own their own boats. This situation continued well into nationalisation, when the GWR became BR (Western Region). At the time I saw them (1949), the boats which had originally been built as fly boats for the Shroppie were old, but beautifully maintained, and had the most beautiful lines of any narrow boat I have ever seen. These fly boats were horse drawn, but an important integral part of British Rail's competitive system.

When Jim and I decided that we would go two-handed we also agreed that I should be in charge of the cooking and catering, and that this should continue for a while, even if we found another hand.

The tunnels on the Staffordshire and Worcestershire - Dunsley and Cookley - are quite short, 65 yards or so, but they are exceedingly small in bore; eight feet eight inches headroom and eight feet two inches wide. There is a towpath in both of them. Our next problem was that we got stuck in Cookley Tunnel, just to the north of Kidderminster. With such a narrow tunnel we had only six inches or so clearance on either beam, so there was not really room to roll the boat and so get clear of whatever it was that was stopping us. We were thankful for the towpaths, for it meant that we could bring the horse into the tunnel, and he eventually pulled us through. The sticking must have been due to the lack of water, as the depth here was at the most only four feet. Whatever the cause, we got free and pressed on and I got on with the cooking. Then just as we got to Kidderminster Lock, disaster struck. I was opening a tin of spiced ham when I sliced open the top of my right thumb on the tin: it was very deep. Although we always carried a first aid box on *Columba* , I did not think of that, and as soon as we were in the lock I staggered off the boat. Luckily, this was one of those locks with a lock-keeper and he had a first aid box out and dealt with the injury in no time. He made me sit down in the Toll Office for a while, and I think I passed out briefly. Poor Jim was very concerned, but after a lengthy delay I recovered sufficiently for us to move on. The major problem was that my right hand was practically useless. Fortunately it did not seem inclined to bleed over much, but I was concerned at the bit of flapping flesh at the top of my thumb, so I kept it tightly bandaged, which meant that I had to use my hand as little as possible. I still have a bulge at the top of my thumb as a souvenir of that spiced ham.

We stayed in the basin at Stourport that night in the midst of those magnificent Brindley warehouses with their clock tower. We also examined the two sets of locks, one broad and one narrow, down into the River Severn. Near here was the intended entry of the Kington and Leominster or the North Hereford Canal, referred to in Tom Rolt's book *Narrow Boat*.

"Only the central portion of the canal was ever opened for traffic, coal from the pits at Mamble being conveyed from Firth Common Wharf to Tenby and Leominster. The great Pensax Tunnel and the flight of locks which were to bring the canal to the Severn above the Stourport bridge were never completed so the canal remained isolated. Had it reached Kington a tramway was to have been constructed from thence to Eardisley in Herefordshire thus forming via the Hay Railway a connection with the Brecon and Abergavenny Canal at Whatton Wharf. Southnet Tunnel and the legendary Pensax Tunnel have been almost totally forgotten, even in the locality, and they are difficult to discover. An afternoon's search in the Teme Valley brought to light the eastern portal of Pensax. Contemporary authorities disagree as to what had been actually accomplished before work on Pensax Tunnel was abandoned and it is probable that it has vanished completely. There is a local legend that the tunnel suddenly collapsed and that the men working there in the shaft at the time are still buried there with their tools beside them. Some Teme Valley people, however, maintain that the story applies to Southnet Tunnel. Certainly the west end of Southnet, if it ever existed, has disappeared."

It was to prove a difficult canal to cut, 45 miles long with a fall from Kington of 496 feet, 207 of which were to have been the fall in a flight of locks at Stourport, possibly even greater in size than Hatton. Southnet Tunnel was to have been 1,250 yards long, but at 3,850 yards, Pensax would have been the second longest tunnel in the country, longer than Sapperton (3,808 yards) on the Thames and Severn and surpassed only by Standedge (5,415 yards) on the Huddersfield Narrow Canal. It so happens that I have a family interest in the Kington and Leominster, because the canal was to have started at Kington, just five miles from my ancestral home at Knill, in Herefordshire. There are still traces in the Kington area of the tram road and between Kington and Eardisley there is still a Tram Inn. I also have a family interest in the canal in the Pensax area, because over the centuries, some members of my family migrated to Tedstone Delamere near Bromyard, just south of Pensax. More recently, my sons went to school at Lucton, just north of Leominster, and in this area are important remains, including the bed of the canal for several miles, road bridges, the remains of a flight of locks and two out of the three arches of a magnificent brick aqueduct across the River Teme, the centre arch having been demolished by the Royal Engineers as a training exercise during the war.

We went down onto the River Severn the next morning and turned downstream to the D & IWE wharf as it then was, just below the power station and above Lincombe Lock. This was another of those excellent wartime innovations, the buffer depot, which did so much to revive the canals, but soon to be rendered unnecessary by the arbitrary denationalisation of road transport with no controlling factors whatsoever. We tied up alongside the high piles of the wharf and waited for our cargo to be craned out, which took about six hours. This great length of time was mainly due to the fact that as soon as a lorry appeared, unloading of boats stopped immediately and the lorry was attended to. Road transport always had priority. Boats with perhaps only half an hour's unloading still to do were often kept waiting for hours or even days, whilst the lorries commanded the complete attention of the staff. Of course, one dared not unload oneself; a strike would have taken place immediately. I could never understand the logic of this, or why the canal carriers did not make more of a protest at the unfairness of such action. The Trade Union was clearly not interested. Because of the anomaly of membership, boatmen were in a small sub-section of the Transport and General Workers Union, whilst the lorry drivers and the wharf men were in a much larger section of the same Union. Majorities had no interest in the rights of minorities. Nobody was going to rock the boat by supporting the boatmen against the other more powerful sections. I often think that this was another reason for the disappearance of the Number One, simply because his turn-round times were obstructed by the unreasonable amount of time taken to load and discharge his cargo.

It would be a magnificent achievement, long overdue, if someone were to put together a history of the Number One. Before the war there had been many distributed over the whole canal network. Amongst these were Charlie Ballinger on the River Severn and Worcester and Birmingham Canals; Joe Skinner on the Oxford and Coventry Canals; Jack Doughty of the *Unostentatious* (surely in view of her dazzling paint work and all-over roses and castles, one of the most curiously named craft ever); the Hones of *White City* and *Cylgate* and *Rose and Betty* (I remember *Cylgate* in my times operated by Samuel Barlow Coal Company, to whom no doubt the Hones had been compelled to sell out); John Hayward in the *Searchlight*; the Townsends of Abingdon; and the Beauchamps of Oxford and very many more.

There were also Charles and Daphne Marsh and their narrow boat, *Heather Belle*. This boat was specially built by the Nurser Brothers at Braunston prior to the war. She was an interesting craft, a motor boat with an additional forward cabin. Early in the war, or just before, the two Marshes (if I remember correctly, he was a solicitor in Worcester) started a scheme for training young ladies in the art of handling narrow boats. One of the first of these girls to finish her training was Kit Gayford, who subsequently worked full-time on the Grand Union. At the beginning of hostilities she was asked by the Ministry of

Transport, who took on the canals, to undertake the training of the girl crews who were recruited on the various schemes they devised. These girls were mainly deployed on the Grand Union.

My late wife, Martin, volunteered for this work, long before we were married, but was turned down because of a "dicky" heart. She subsequently volunteered for, and was accepted by, the Guide International Service, and became a team leader in the Girl Guide movement in Denmark, Holland and Germany, as the war was coming to a close. Another volunteer for the canals was Sonia South, who became the wife of George Smith, the skipper of Samuel Barlow's boats *Cairo* and *Warwick*, and who later married Tom Rolt.

By the time I started in 1948, of those mentioned only Charlie Ballinger and Joe Skinner were still working as Number Ones, with two or three others. Later, Tom Foxon bought one of my boats and became a Number One himself. This boat, originally called the *Hesperus*, I had renamed *Chad*. Tom changed her name once again, this time to *New Hope*. Recently, she has undergone a refit, and her name has been changed back to *Hesperus*. She is now owned by David Blagrove, author of *Bread Upon the Waters* and is once again used for carrying.

I feel that I cannot do better at this point than to quote again from Tom Rolt's *Narrow Boat*:

> "Number One is the canal term for a boat, owned by her captain, as distinct from those owned by canal carrying companies, which are worked by paid crews. In the past the bulk of the canal traffic was handled by these independents, the carrying company being a comparatively recent development, but modern conditions are all against the old race of owner-boatmen. Possessing no capital reserve to see them through a slack spell, and unable to draw dole allowance, they cannot survive the cut-throat competition of the modern haulage business. Many have given up the unequal struggle by selling their boats and their labours to one or another of the companies, and so - more is the pity - there are few Number Ones left on the canals now ...."

It used to be said that if you scratched a Grand Union captain that you found a Number One, or one that was descended from one.

So we eventually unloaded our cargo. There was no hope of any return loading from Stourport, so we decided to go down to Worcester and see what we could do from there. We went down the River Severn and made remarkably good time. It was interesting to see how fast a small Woolwich boat with an eighteen horse-power engine, running single and light, could really go. I should imagine that we must have been doing about 12 to 15 miles per hour over the bottom which, even allowing for the amount of the current, was a very good speed.

We had a beautiful run down to Worcester, 13 miles and three locks, which we covered in about two hours on a lovely late summer's evening. We tied up in Diglis Basin. Next day we contacted the D & IWE office in Worcester and ascertained that there was no chance of any loading, so we decided to leave the next day for Brum. Whilst in Worcester I acquired a rather nice original horse-brass - I think I paid 7s 6d for it. It had a representation of a paddle steamer on it and (I thought) the letters on it to be C.W.S. At first I could not make out the connection between the Co-operative Wholesale Society and paddle steamers. On closer study the first letter was revealed to be a G - so of course the correct interpretation was the Great Western Steamship Company, and the whole thing made sense.

Jim and I agreed to approach Brum by way of the Worcester and Birmingham Canal. This canal had a somewhat chequered early history, having had no less than four engineers. Construction began in 1791 at the Birmingham end, to the line originally surveyed by John Snape and Josiah Clowes. There were immediate difficulties. On the canal there is a fall all the way to Worcester, with no way to recover the lost water; the Birmingham Canals refused to let them have water except under the most stringent conditions, and in fact had a clause put in their Bill to the effect that the Worcester and Birmingham should come no nearer than seven feet to any canal in the Birmingham system. This accounts for the infamous Worcester Bar - the name survives to this day. As a result the engineering works were vast, no less than 10 spring-fed reservoirs being dug. This had more tunnels for its length, and probably for any length, in the country. By 1794 the cutting of the Kings Norton Tunnel had begun, but because of its length it was not opened for 13 years in 1807, and the boats could only cover the 13½ miles to Tardebigge Wharf, by which time four tunnels and 30 over-bridges had been negotiated. Here, for financial and engineering reasons, work came to a stop for several years, eventually to start again under a new engineer. This was John Woodhouse, who favoured lifts, thus reducing the number of locks from 78 to 12. The company was not enthusiastic, and limited his experiments to one, hence the depth of Tardebigge Lock at 14 feet. The directors were not happy and called in a new engineer, John Rennie, who decided that the lifts would not stand the wear and tear, and installed locks, but now reduced to the number of 58.

However, after the short history of the canal and its troubles, we must get back to Worcester. The two of us had now to see what sort of a fist we could make of those 58 locks, especially the 31 up Tardebigge. I was curious to see this particular route because the Worcester and Birmingham formed the fourth arm of the canals centred on Birmingham - what boatmen called 'The Cross' -and was the only one we had not travelled so far. It was not used much. We had previously been to the northern end of the canal when I went to Cadbury's to load chocolate crumb, but it was the first time I had had the opportunity to travel its full length. We found it on the whole rather shallow, which perhaps accounted for the fact that there was not much traffic on it.

Those 58 locks are all situated in the first 15½ miles from Worcester, which averages out at one every quarter mile, in fact as a foretaste of what was to come, there are six locks within the city area. My remembrance over approximately 35 years is that there was not much of interest until we got to the foot of the Lickey Hills and the Tardebigge Tunnel (568 yards long) and the flight of locks, but first there was Dunhampstead Tunnel through which the boats were pulled by means of a handrail fixed to the wall. (Fortunately the tunnel was only 326 yards long.) I say not much of interest and trust my words will not be taken amiss by the supporters of the Worcester and Birmingham, but I was comparing it with the stark engineering of the Liverpool and Birmingham and the "cosiness" of the Staffordshire and Worcestershire. The other two canals that join the Worcester and Birmingham at its lower end were then completely derelict with apparently no hope of rebirth *[but were in fact restored in 2010/11]*. I refer of course to the Droitwich and Droitwich Junction Canals.

The Tardebigge flight is the canal equivalent of the Lickey Incline, which caused such problems for the Midland Railway in its early days. The steepness of the ascent made it necessary to design and build special banking engines, and even today with the advent of the 125, it is unlikely that more than seven coaches will be achieved without a drastic increase in horse-power. There is a magnificent view down into Worcestershire from the top lock, from where it is possible to appreciate the steepness of the ascent. As my eye moved across the timeless landscape, I was reminded that just out in these hills, in the year 820, was martyred the infant King of Mercia, St Kenelm, after whom I later named one of my boats.

It was at the wharf at the top of Tardebigge flight that Tom Rolt moored *Cressy* whilst he was working for the Ministry of Supply from May 1941 until 1944. He and his first wife Angela were to remain here until the end of the war. It was also from here that *Narrow Boat* was published in December 1944. It was very well received, with runaway sales instead of the rebuffs and rejections of the previous two-and-a-half years. Here too, shortly after the book was published, Tom Rolt and Robert Aickman met for the first time. The meeting led to the formation of the Inland Waterways Association and there is now a plaque on the canal bank commemorating the event.

The next tunnel after leaving Tardebigge was Shortwood Tunnel (608 yards). Six miles further on lay the West or Wast Hill Tunnel at Kings Norton. This tunnel was a major proposition with a length of 2,750 yards. Horse-boats, of which there were very few, were hauled through by a tug. The main user in 1949 was Charlie Ballinger, the Number One from Gloucester. After leaving Wast Hill Tunnel it was a matter of five miles to Worcester Bar, then down Farmer's Bridge Locks (13), down Ashtead (6) and up Camp Hill (6) and we were back to Sherborne Street and then to Tyseley to collect *Uranus*, back to Hawkesbury Stop empty and then to Newdigate to load for Croxley.

More changes were on the way. For some time I had been aware of the fact that Jim had been courting, but I suppose I had not given much thought to the possible consequences of this. His girl was called Rose Monk and she came from a boating family, too. At this time the family was working a Samuel Barlow pair, the motor being the *Hardy*, but I regret to say that after all these years the name of the butty escapes me. It was an unusual set-up, because the boat's working captain was Rose's mother. This uncommon situation came about because Rose's father had become invalided, so her mother took over. Rose had a brother called Henry who looked after the engine although father was sometimes called upon for advice when the others could not cope. Jim had known Rose before he joined me, and had spent a lot of time with her during the six weeks when *Columba* and *Uranus* were laid up, so I suppose I should have come as no surprise when Jim announced that he and Rose were to be married before long. So, in November, Jim left me and, after his marriage, got a pair of narrow boats of his own. Later he went to work for the British Waterways, but 'on the bank' as canal people say.

With the departure of Jim, I think it is best to pause and take stock. The 15 months or so that Jim had been with me had taught me a vast amount about the handling of a pair of boats that was important, but he had, I think, probably more importantly, also taught me an awful lot about being, thinking and behaving like a boatman. In spite of my age when I started, 35, that year had matured and developed me in a way that I had never achieved before. I could go on, but I want you to read this, not throw it down in disgust. What I am leading up to is that I felt I had an obligation to Jim, to remember what he had taught me, to be proud of what I had learnt and to carry on as before after he had gone. This is probably why some of the chaps who came to work for me in after years found me to be too fussy, too much of a stickler, but I had learnt that my boats were my home and my tools and they must be treated as such, capable of giving the instant response which they would not be able to give if they were not in apple pie order. Yes, I was and ever will be grateful to Jim. I only regret that our ways parted, and I that I was not to see him until recently, once he left the cut. He asked me to attend his Wedding and I was to have gone with my wife, because by this time I was married too, but Martin was too ill and we could not attend.

I had been very kindly and sincerely treated by Jim's large family, as indeed I was by all the boatmen with whom I came into contact. I found this again two years later when a young Wally James came to work for me. He carried on from where Jim had stopped and I got to know and like his parents and family as well. But that was to be in 1951, and we are now at the end of 1949.

Chapter Five

A NEW CREW MEMBER

Jim's departure meant that I could not possibly work the boats single-handed. It was extremely difficult to get boys or young chaps of any kind of standard that I wanted on the Grand Union. They were just not around because so many boatmen were leaving the cut, and those that were staying were generally required by the family boats to keep them going. At this point, August 1949, this paragraph appeared in the Inland Waterways Association's Bulletin.

> "Our Junior Member, Mr L. T. Foxon (aged 17)... would like employment to do with the waterways. He would prefer the open air, but office work would not be objected to. Mr Foxon has obtained his School Certificate. We feel that some of our members may be glad to obtain the services of a youthful enthusiast who wishes to make a career with the waterways. Those interested should write direct to Mr. Foxon."

Tom Foxon was at this time working in an insurance office in Reading, where his family lived, but he was dead keen on the cut and boats, and offered to come and work for me. His parents were quite willing, and I thought this was a thing not to be passed over, so I went down to Reading to see him. We had lunch, but I cannot remember where - it was one of those restaurants similar to Lyon's Corner House which used to be so common, and where the waitresses always wore black dresses and white aprons. I do remember I had a curry. Anyhow, we had a good talk about ways and means and it was agreed that he should come and work for me on the boats, starting after Christmas 1949.

The consideration that decided me to take Tom Foxon, in spite of his ignorance of how to handle a boat were: firstly, he had great keenness; secondly, I had learned to handle a boat and was sure that he could; thirdly, his undoubted experience of office work meant that he would probably be able to master my rampant filing system; and finally that he had a really staggering knowledge of traffics and canals. I think he read my Bradshaw from cover to cover, but more soon.

His coming to work for me more or less saved the situation, even though it meant that until he was trained I felt I could no longer operate on the Grand Union Canal, as we just would not be able to cope with the butty. I decided to leave *Uranus* in the ex-Fellows Morton transfer shed at Braunston, where Tom was going to join me, as I had decided to take the motor boat up onto the Shropshire Union Canal and to do sub-contract work for D & IWE in the north and east, that is on the Shropshire Union, the Staffordshire and Worcestershire and the Trent and Mersey. We hoped there would be plenty of cargo up there.

Going north as we were from Braunston, we had the choice of two routes, Grand Union or bottom road. We decided to go the bottom road, spending the first night at Hawkesbury Stop (22 miles and 3 locks) rather than the Grand Union, as we reckoned that with just the motor boat, the single locks would be easier to work than the double ones up Hatton, and the others. So we went via the Coventry Canal to Fazeley Junction, where again we had a choice. We could have carried on to Fradley Junction and then up the Trent and Mersey to the Potteries and Harecastle Tunnel, but this was a bit of an uncertainty, especially with a green mate. So we went by the Birmingham and Fazeley to Salford Junction, then up the eleven locks of the Aston flight and the thirteen of the Farmer's Bridge flight, which took us on to the Birmingham level, by which time we had come up 116 feet. The Birmingham level of the Birmingham Canal Navigations (or BCN) had been built by Thomas Telford to supplement Smeaton's original main line *[actually, Brindley's, later improved by Smeaton]*. Telford used deep cuttings and massive embankments, just as he had done on the Shropshire Union; he also shortened the distance between Birmingham and Wolverhampton by cutting out the Soho and Oozells Street loops, amongst other short cuts, thus reducing the distance to the top of Farmer's Bridge Lock from 21 to 13 miles, and with only three locks to be negotiated at Factory Junction in Tipton, which is just over half-way from Birmingham.

Fast passenger boats used to operate along Telford's improved canal. They were lightweight, built of wrought iron, and of narrow beam with covered accommodation, similar to a modern bus in layout. They were probably about 60 feet long and pulled by four or possibly six horses. They worked on the principle of using the primary wave. Telford's Birmingham canals were virtually straight, shallow (able to accommodate craft with a draft of about three feet six inches) and not over-wide, although wide enough to allow two craft of seven foot beam to pass each other easily. A boat passing along such a canal acts as a piston, pushing a wave perhaps 9 to 18 inches high in front of it. Starting off at a pace

Columba and *Lucy* at top lock, Braunston, in 1952 or 1953. The new signwriting reflects the birth of son Thomas in August 1952. His mother, Martin, is second from right, on the towpath.

that would be increased to a slow trot, the wave would be pushed ahead of the boat; the horses would then be whipped to a gallop, which would jerk the boat forward and lift it on to the primary wave, thereby increasing the draught of the canal from three foot six to perhaps four foot six inches or more at the wave as it moved along the canal. The extra speed now achieved by the boat automatically increased the speed of the wave, friction was thus reduced and the horses could maintain a speed of perhaps 12 miles per hour to their first change, which would probably be at the Junction already mentioned at Tipton. The journey from Birmingham to Wolverhampton of 13½ miles could be undertaken in between one and two hours, according to the conditions and the number of changes.

A similar scheme was in operation between Bath (Darlington Wharf) and Bradford-on-Avon on the Kennet and Avon Canal. The Bath boats also had a string band on board, and light refreshments were served. The fare was ls 6d and the journey time one hour for the nine miles.

I seem to remember that we tied up at the top of the Minworth flight that night. It had been a long day. I expect Tom wondered what he had let himself in for. Next day he would know, because we got to the top of Wolverhampton flight (27 locks and 20 miles). Not bad - 76½ miles and 58 locks in three days.

So we plunged down the Wolverhampton flight, a drop of about 120 feet in one and a quarter miles, from the heaviest of Black Country industry at the summit to the sylvan surroundings of the foot. Here too is the junction with the Staffordshire and Worcestershire at Aldersley Junction, so the circle was made from when I had last passed this junction nearly six months before.

We then turned left at Autherley Junction to a friendly greeting of recognition from Sam Lomas the toll clerk, who helped us through the stop lock. Then up to Wheaton Aston and whilst Tom looked after *Columba*, I renewed my acquaintance with the Post-Mistress. What a delightful shop that was at Wheaton Aston, with the most delicious smell, a sort of melange of tea, coffee, spice, fresh bread, smoked bacon and apples. After a snack lunch we moved on to Gnosall and tied up for the night. Then early next morning we were off again.

This is a really wonderful canal and on this second trip I was more able to appreciate the impressiveness of the engineering, the deep cuttings, the height of the embankments and above all, the directness of the line. There was the delightful corniced and balustraded bridge near Wheaton Aston. There were the high bridges in Woodseaves cutting; impressive singly, but two in line seem to accentuate even more Telford's genius. There was the charm of the little tunnel at Cowley, just 80 yards long, but with a towpath.

We passed on, joining the Chester Canal Navigation at Nantwich Basin, then past Hurleston Junction, turning right at Barbridge Junction and tying up at Cholmondeston on the Middlewich Branch of the Shropshire Union Canal. We set off again the next morning along the Wardle Lock Branch of the Trent and Mersey Canal, to join the canal at Middlewich. We were now on the canal that Brindley had called the Grand Trunk, but these days it is normally referred to as the Trent and Mersey. It is unusual, some people think, for Brindley in that it is quite level for 17 miles from Middlewich. Even this pales into insignificance however; on reaching its end, you turn into the Duke's Cut or Bridgewater at Waters Meeting, and find that it has a pound 40 miles in length - unsurpassed on any British canal.

I have said that the Trent and Mersey was one of Brindley's canals, in actual fact it was the Brindley canal, the key to the whole canal system that he had so brilliantly conceived. I have mentioned the "cross" earlier, but have perhaps not given it the importance that was due to it. This I shall now try to do. I have referred to the Bridgewater Canal, which was the work which began the modern canal revolution, linking as it did the cities and towns of Lancashire and Northern Cheshire with the Duke of Bridgewater's collieries at Worsley.

The young Duke of Bridgewater went on the Grand Tour of Europe in the late 1730s; towards the end of the trip he visited the south of France and saw the Canal du Midi, constructed in the seventeenth century to join the Mediterranean Sea to the Atlantic Ocean. This showed him how he might implement his father's ideas of moving coal from the collieries. On his return to England he was introduced to millwright James Brindley, aged 46, self taught and practically illiterate *[it is now known that he was not]* , but showing a natural genius and a man of terrific resource. He showed the Duke how a canal could be dug from Worsley to Manchester along which it would be possible to transport the coal, instead of moving it by horse and cart along the terrible roads of the time. An Act of Parliament was obtained in 1759 and the work started. It was completed in 1761 - in spite of natural obstacles of the River Irwell at Barton and Trafford Moss, both involving long embankments. Brindley, countering strong arguments to the contrary, showed how these could be made watertight by his use of puddle. Brindley demonstrated before a House of Commons committee that when water is poured on to dry clay it runs quickly through, but mix the dry clay with water, moulding or puddling it with the hands, and it will retain water which is poured into the finished puddle as long as it is moist. Brindley's canal into Manchester was dead level and only 10½ miles long. The price of coal in Manchester fell by 10 shillings a ton overnight. The canal was then extended to Runcorn where there was a flight of locks down to the Irwell and the sea. The canal was now 28 miles long and capable of accepting craft with a beam of up to 15 feet and a length of 72 feet, even through the locks to the Irwell, and for 27 miles of its total length was level. But more was to come.

Such was the success of the Duke's Cut in fostering trade and reducing prices that Brindley produced his plans for joining the Rivers Thames, Severn, Mersey and Trent, and then the Humber as well, by navigable waterways. The first of these was the Grand Trunk, to run from the Duke's Cut near Runcorn at Preston Brook to the Midlands in the form of a flat "V" to the Trent. Next to come was the Staffordshire and Worcestershire from Fradley on the Trent and Mersey, then the Oxford Canal. The whole was to be tied together with a network around Birmingham and the Black Country. Hence the "cross". It was all to be completed, but not entirely in Brindley's lifetime. There were to be obstacles, as one would expect with the work force which the times imposed, but the greatest obstacle of all was the central watershed at Harecastle. Brindley proposed piercing a tunnel 2,897 yards long. Whilst not the longest in the country, it was, at the time, of a length that had never been attempted before. Local pundits called it "Brindley's Air Castle". The tunnel had no towpath, the boats having to be legged through. Alas, Brindley died in 1772 at the age of 56. All was in use except the Harecastle Tunnel (finished in 1777) and the Oxford Canal (completed in 1790).

So we might be forgiven for regarding our present position with a certain amount of awe. I know Tom did; I perhaps was a little more blasé. Be that as it may, we tied up that night at Anderton, just above the famous lift. Below was the River Weaver and the Winnington Works of the ICI. This had once been the Mond Chemical Works, founded by Sir Alfred Mond, until taken over by the larger concern in about 1925. My mother had a friend who married Egbert James, then working in the offices of the Mond Chemical Company. The family disapproved strongly at her choosing such an obscure husband. He subsequently became Chairman of ICI and Town Clerk of Northwich.

I went down the next morning and ordered five gallons of lubricating oil from the Shell Nantwich agent. Nobody seemed to know anything about loading at the Lift Office, so I decided to pay a visit to Liverpool, where the Docks and Inland Waterways Executive had their office, in Dale Street as far as I, remember, the office of the North Western Division.

I arrived in Liverpool, having travelled by train and bus, and was shown into the office of Christopher Marsh, who was at that time the Divisional Waterways Officer. He was very pleased to see me and after a talk suggested that I went to see his Divisional Sales Officer, Mr C. S. R. Hall.

I went to see Mr Hall and was given a glass of sherry. I had a very good talk with him and was able to tell him of my experiences and about my boats; how I was capable of carrying any grade of cargo in *Columba* and *Uranus*, although owing to manning problems only *Columba* was operational at the time, but that she alone could carry up to 25 tons of suitable cargo, given the water.

It seemed that there was no loading for a few days but that the D & IWE were very glad to have me up there for a few months, as they were expecting a lot of traffic which had been held up by the Atlantic storms. He suggested that I should lay at Anderton for the time being, which would be convenient for loading either at the bottom of the lift, the cargo coming up the Weaver in flats, or at Runcorn, or even Manchester Docks. I decided that it would be safe to go home for a couple of days as Tom was quite competent and safe to be left in charge of the boat. I set off.

I got home to find that there had been a telephone call from Mr Hall whom I had seen only two or three days before; apparently he had tried to get me at Anderton, but I had already left. He had rung more than once, but would ring again the following morning. Mr Hall was as good as his word, and early mid-morning of the following day he rang again. The line was pretty bad, but it transpired that Newbury Laundry wanted 20 tons of salt delivered by canal and I was to be at the Cerebos factory in Middlewich first thing on the morning of Monday, 6th February 1950.

Chapter Six

THE FIRST SALT RUN

It seemed now that my talks some time before with John Gould and John Lester and the more recent ones with Mr Hall had borne fruit and we were soon to set out on what was for us a great adventure. I felt, and I think Tom did too, that the voyage of Jason and the Argonauts was as nothing compared with what our journey would be. Like Jason we did not know what the problems and indeed the dangers which lay ahead of us were. When Mr Hall rang, he had informed me that 20 tons of salt were to be transported from the Middlewich factory of Cerebos Ltd. to Newbury on the Kennet and Avon Canal. John Lester of the Newbury Laundry normally obtained his salt from Cerebos and had made this arrangement with their agent, Mr Cranston. John was one of the small band of people in Newbury who saw a future in the Kennet and Avon Canal. Little did any of us realise that this enthusiasm had been falsely fuelled through the duplicity of the Docks and Inland Waterways Executive, and would involve them in a case in the High Court which would cost them thousands of pounds and set the future of the canal back 30 years. Within 15 years or so, those stretches of the canal that we had passed along so comparatively easily would have assumed the appearance of open fields ripe for the reaping, purely through the intentional neglect of the statutory Nationalised Authority which was supposed to be maintaining them, but more of this at the proper time.

This was the gist of our orders. We were to load at Cerebos on Friday 10th February at nine-thirty in the morning. The factory would help us load the salt, and the cargo was to be sheeted up the whole time. We were to receive assistance from the NW Division as far as Fradley, the worst part of the run, and we should be granted a special low through-toll, except for the river section, Oxford to Reading, which was under Thames Conservancy control. I gave my estimate of the time this trip would take as about 10 to 14 days.

We set to work planning the trip, again turning to my old Bradshaw. Owing to the necessity of going through the Harecastle Tunnel and fitting in with the times of the tug, which was the obligatory method of passage, the Trent and Mersey would have to be divided into two sections.

The Cerebos factory was situated alongside the canal to the south of Middlewich. Loading would be across the towpath, so the Cerebos gang pushed the sacks in wheelbarrows to the bank, and Tom and I lowered them into the boat and stacked them. The salt was not the kind you have on your table, but rather crude salt which is put into machines to soften water in laundry work. The salt mines around Middlewich are huge, the caverns running many miles underground. On one famous occasion in 1844, at Marston not far away, the Tsar of Russia, his entourage and members of the Royal Society were all entertained to an enormous banquet underground in the mine, which was lit by thousands of lamps in honour of the event.

The distance from Cerebos to the north end of Harecastle Tunnel was 13 miles with 30 locks, so much depended on how quickly we could finish loading and be sheeted up. Tom was new to this, so most of the burden fell on me and we prayed that the weather, which was overcast, would remain dry. Loading with the very helpful Cerebos gang was finished by twelve-thirty, we were sheeted up by one-thirty and away, after a meal, by two-o'clock. We tied up that night below Lock 55, the second of Pierpoints flight, very late. We had come only nine miles and through 14 locks, so we were up very early again the next morning, ready for the remaining four miles and 16 locks to bring us to the north end of Harecastle Tunnel.

A number of these locks we found to be paired or double locks, which had the object of saving water. To empty the lock, you used the centre paddles so that some (about half) of the water drained into the sister lock rather than into the canal, so that effectively this water was used twice. Another boat coming downhill would only need half a lock of extra water in order to make the descent.

Locks 65 and 66 were the Wheelock Locks, a name known to practically every boatman because it was here that the famous Wheelock windlasses were made by the lock-keeper, a cottage industry. It was possible to buy a windlass here to fit almost every paddle spindle in the country. They were all stamped with the trade mark of the craftsman, a clay pipe. At one time I had three of these windlasses, a Grand Union, an Oxford and a Trent and Mersey. Sadly they were all lost or stolen after a talk I had given about the Kennet and Avon at Swindon.

We arrived at the Tunnel to find that we had just missed the tug, and queued up for the one at three forty-five under a lowering sky. As I remember it, there were three or four boats ahead of us, and we were "Tail-end Charlie". This might give us problems, as a motor boat is notoriously difficult to handle when the engine is not in use, and I could not help thinking how much better it would be to have someone behind us. During our enforced wait of some two and a half hours I could not help ruminating on the condition of my business at that time, and assessing how we were progressing. Our trip from Braunston to Anderton had been something of a pleasure cruise, but now we were having to work to a timetable and conditions imposed upon us by others from which we could not diverge; but Tom was shaping up very nicely under this pressure.

On Brindley's original canal he had built a tunnel at Harecastle which was only wide enough to take a single boat, and had no towpath; in 1804 its headroom was only five feet ten inches. As traffic increased, this tunnel became a terrible bottleneck, so Telford was asked to cut a second tunnel parallel to it, 2,919 yards long, with headroom of eight feet ten inches and a cantilevered towpath throughout its length. The tunnels were then the canal equivalent of a dual carriageway until 1914, when mining subsidence had caused Brindley's tunnel to sink so much that it became unusable. Then electric haulage was installed in Telford's tunnel. According to my Bradshaw, if the tug stopped working, boatmen were supposed to bow-haul through, using the towpath.

I was aroused from my musings by movement ahead of us, and judged that the tug must be about due. By this time another horse boat had arrived, so we would not be last and this would make our passage easier. The tug picked up its power from an overhead cable like a tram-car, but with two wires, and it also picked up a chain from the bottom of the canal which was drawn over a toothed drum in the bottom of the hull, thus pulling itself along. The passage time with six boats seemed to be about half to three-quarters of an hour.

It was very eerie gliding through this underworld in darkness except for the lights of our own and other cabins illuminating the old, soot-covered brickwork of the tunnel roof. By this dim light we could see that Telford's tunnel was sinking too through mining subsidence, and that the towpath was completely under water in places, so *Bradshaw's* advice about bow-hauling was outdated. We wondered how long this tunnel would last and whether, when the time came another tunnel would be cut, or if that would be the end.

We cleared the tunnel at about half past four, by which time it was just getting dark - and it was pouring down with rain. It had been a disappointing day as far as distance travelled, but with having to wait for the tug it could not have been otherwise. Within a short distance of the tunnel we tied up, in our innocence expecting to make Great Haywood the next night. It was, after all, only 22 miles and 18 locks, and during the day we had covered four miles and 16 locks as well as hanging around for the tug for several hours, in which time we should have travelled another 12 miles.

John Knill tying up *Columba* (left), probably to *Kenelm*.

We left early the next morning, by which time, fortunately, the rain had stopped. Four miles later we arrived at the wharves of the Anderton Company and their boat dock at Middleport. We found that there were no D & IWE boats working here. The principal carriers of pottery, material were Potter and Son of Runcorn, and the Mersey Weaver and Anderton Companies. China clay and other materials were brought from Cornwall and Scandinavia to Weston Point on the Weaver Navigation and to Runcorn Docks. From there they were traditionally carried by narrow boat to the individual works in the Potteries, but this unfortunately succumbed to competition from road transport from about 1950 onwards. Other carriers using the canal, according to our observations, were John Walley and J & G Meakin and some others.

Suddenly we were in a scene that seemed to be out of Dante's *Inferno*, or perhaps Lang's *Metropolis*. It was the Shelton Steel Works, with the canal running through the middle. We were having trouble with rubbish in the water and the next thing that happened was that we had lost way - a sheer-pin had gone, thus disconnecting the propeller from the engine. I realised that we were out of spares, because in the general excitement, replacing them had been overlooked, so we shafted *Columba* into the bank. I then went off in search of replacements. The people in the steel works were most helpful and after about half an hour, going to various workshops, I eventually came away with half a dozen new sheer-pins. One was installed and we were off again, down towards Trentham, which was virtually the southern-most limit of regular traffic on the canal. This fact was soon demonstrated by the shallowness of the water, and the resultant slow progress meant that we had to face the abandonment of the timetable I had thought possible. There did not seem to be any likelihood of attaining the kind of speeds I had estimated until we reached Fradley Junction, still 27 miles away, but we thought we might be able to make up for lost time by working another late night. We tied up that night at Sandon, after 18 miles and 15 locks. We had been travelling now for three days and had covered 33 miles and 46 locks, not what I would call from previous experience a sparkling performance. The weather was bad and the conditions were worse. We now did not see any other boats at all and we were continually encountering bad scours, and what perhaps was worse, a basic shallowness. Although officially the depth should have been four feet, my estimation was that we were only drawing about three feet six inches and we were also on the bottom.

At last we came to Great Haywood Junction, where the northern section of the Staffordshire and Worcestershire Canal joined. There are two very notable bridges here, one by Brindley which has a beautiful flat arch in brick and the other a magnificent pack-horse bridge of mediaeval date over the River Trent. So slow had been our progress that it was now quite late in the day.

Just after getting dark and as we were leaving Colwich Lock, I was mesmerised by the sight of a row of brilliant lights which gave me the impression that we were travelling at immense speed. I have found that it is often possible to get hallucinations in the dark, such as the, feeling that the canal is running downhill (which happened to me once above Stone as I was entering Newshill Locks - most disturbing). Well, here we were apparently going to collide with something because of the great speed at which we were travelling. I then came to, and realised that it was not us going at a great speed, but the lights themselves. Only then did the full realisation dawn that we were running alongside the London, Midland and Scottish main line and that the lighted, noisy monster that was bearing down on us at 20 times our own speed was the night mail and that we were just going under a railway bridge, which was why it appeared to be either swallowing us or about to run us down. We had a brief glimpse of what appeared to be a massive Duchess Class Pacific. A thundering roar, a flash of light, a rapidly-receding tail-light and it was gone. The lights on the coaches were all part of the pick-up and dropping gear of a mail train.

We now went on past Brindley's Bank and by the time we had covered the next mile to Rugeley it was dark and late. Here we came to a complete halt. We were stuck fast outside what we soon discovered was a tannery. The pong was absolutely appalling. After trying to get free for the best part of an hour we decided to stay for the night and see what we could do next day in daylight. As we were in the middle of the canal and unable to get ashore, we did not actually tie up at all. There was no doubt that the absence of any through traffic had allowed the build-up of a huge scour, caused in this case by waste discharged from the tannery. So we were down to about 10 miles and about 10 locks again, and four days out, leaving only between 6 and 10 days for the rest of the journey. It seemed quite impossible that the run could be completed on time. I must have been pretty naive to think we could have done better, but we were falling far short of the D & IWE's assurances on progress. Admittedly, it was in the early days of nationalisation and possibly they had not been able to make a true assessment of what conditions were really like.

It was not particularly pleasant being outside the tannery, but there was nothing we could do about it. We saw one or two people on the towpath; they did not comment, so we concluded that, being local, they had probably got used both to boats being stuck here and to the smell. We were up and about fairly early the next day, hoping that action in daylight would help us to get clear fairly quickly, but it was not to be so. But at long last moving we were, at first very slowly, then at probably under two miles an hour. We crept along, having thankfully waved goodbye to Rugeley.

Suddenly, outside a factory making Armitage Ware, we stuck fast again on a scour of pottery waste. We were fast here until mid-afternoon, and then we moved slowly forward once more, and into Armitage Tunnel, where we once again came to a halt just about the middle of the tunnel. In later years the tunnel was opened out into a cutting, but at the time of our being stuck in it, it had a length of 130 yards, a width at water level of ten feet six inches and a height of 13 feet. There was a towpath. Presumably this was a rubbish bank, or more probably an obstruction caused by lack of dredging. Eventually we got clear and then at Kings Bromley we stuck again. We had been here a little while when we saw several men coming purposively towards us. They turned out to be a canal gang from Fradley Junction, comprising an Inspector and three or four men, headed by Mr Marsh, the Divisional Waterways Officer. Apparently, Fradley had been alerted to our run and when we had not turned up, Mr Marsh had been informed and a search party instituted. Needless to say, he was not very pleased with the furore we had

Jim Jackson

caused and it was suggested that we were somewhat overloaded, to put it mildly. I pointed out that we firstly were not to know the state of the canal and, secondly, that the weight of 20 tons had been agreed by his own Traffic Officer, who had presumably consulted the Engineering Department.

However, with the help of his gang we got clear, and parted on a very friendly basis and soon arrived at Fradley Junction, which we were very pleased to see. Fradley was the southern boundary of the North Western Division, so we were now moving into the territory of the South Eastern Division, from which we expected great things. We went first on to the detached portion of the Coventry Canal, then, by way of Whittington Brook, we entered the Birmingham and Fazeley Canal. At Tamworth we had some bad going again, but we got through without too much trouble to Fazeley Junction. We were now back on waterways which we already knew, as we now took the Coventry Canal main line through Nuneaton to Hawkesbury, and the going was good and remained so. Before the boats were docked we had often been here with Jim Jackson to load coal at Pooley Hall, Polesworth and Baddesley Collieries.

One of the points of interest to me at Baddesley Colliery was that they used locomotives of the Garrett type. One day, whilst waiting to load before going to Hawkesbury Stop, I had been given a ride in one.

Unfortunately we were over-hopeful about our progress and although we never got stuck again, the going was very slow. We spent the night at Glascote Junction, having travelled the five and a half miles of the detached portion of the Coventry Canal and 14¼ miles for the day. We were going to have to work very long hours to make any impression on our backlog. We had so far taken five days for the comparatively short distance we had to date travelled. Our next problem was where to spend the next night, Saturday; whether to stay at Hawkesbury Stop or to press on. It was 26 miles to Hawkesbury, and we had to stop there anyway to top up with fuel at the *Greyhound*, where we could also get food at the *Greyhound* shop. From here to Hawkesbury, all the locks were single and of course in good condition as they were used regularly by the boats serving the Coventry coalfields, and there were at this time over three hundred pairs operating this Division of the D & IWE. However, the actual condition of the canal itself would not improve until we were past Amington at the earliest, and that was two miles away. We finally got to Hawkesbury at about five o'clock. We then fuelled up and went to the shop, so that it was about six o'clock by the time we had finished. Then we tied up for the night and had a wash and a meal.

At one time there was a kind of wild free-for-all for coal orders at Hawkesbury Stop, which was a sort of Clapham Junction of the canals. To ensure that cargoes were more fairly allocated than they were in this haphazard melee, all the carrying companies got together and organised a Boat Control Office, so boatmen could tie up, check in, and be dealt with in a sensible, systematic way. The *Greyhound* pub here was always crammed full with boatmen playing darts or dominoes, or singing and dancing to a melodeon whilst they waited for their orders. Many boatmen would also tie up here for their holidays, or whilst their wives were in the last few days of their pregnancies. Because of the dwindling amount of traffic, the Boat Control Office ceased to exist in 1963.

We proposed making an early start next day, with the intention of getting to the top of Napton before they locked up - 31¼ miles and only nine locks. What a change in conditions; plenty of water, and plenty of boats to talk to as we went: Joshers, Grand Union, Harvey-Taylor, Ovaltine, Samuel Barlow, S E Barlow, George Garside; and we saw Joe Skinner and *Friendship*. He was mighty pleased to know we were taking a cargo down his beloved Oxford Canal. Most of the boatmen seemed pleased to see us and chafed us by asking such questions as, "Have you been on your holidays?". We exchanged all sorts of boatman's chit-chat and they gave us the latest news of Jim and Rose. It was nice, too, to hear the sound of boats - the difference in cadence between a 16 and 18 horse Bolinder, the busy thump of a National or the completely different sound of one of Samuel Barlow's three-cylinder Gardner or Ruston engines.

After the very bad corner at Anstey, which very often used to give me trouble when steering *Uranus*, is one of the lengths of canal straightened out by Telford during the modernisation of the Oxford Canal in the early nineteenth century. This was at Brinklow, where owing to the twisting nature of the canal, it used to be said that you could travel for a whole day and still hear the same church bells. A perusal of a large-scale map will reveal the route followed by Brindley. The original meanders of the waterway, now cut across by the direct line of the new canal, became branches of it in order to keep connections with depots on the old line. Telford employed the same methods which he had used on the Shropshire Union, extending even to massive embankments and cuttings and the tunnel at Newbold. We journeyed on to Hillmorton and its three locks. These were double locks, as we had experienced on the Trent and Mersey. It was salutary to realise that in spite of having been going for the best part of seven days we had only succeeded in covering 77 miles (an average of 11 miles a day) and 71 locks. But with any luck, we should find it possible to make a great improvement on that figure by the time we tied up for the night. More pleasant lengths of canal followed and then we were alongside the old Great Central main railway line for quite a while. It was a change to hear the "Eldrich squeak" of the London and North Eastern locomotives. As nationalisation was barely 18 months old, many things had not yet been standardised, so there was still a contrast between these sounds and the siren-like noise of the old LMS. The story behind the adoption of the ship's siren-like note was that when the Caledonian Railway built their new locomotive *Cardeen* they wanted to give it a sound of its own, so they adopted a whistle with the same sound as the Clyde river steamers. When Sir William Stanier designed his new series of locomotives on taking over as Chief Engineer of the LMS, he decided to use *Cardeen's* whistle on these, too.

Talking of whistles, I suppose the most nerve-tingling, especially at night, was a Great Western high-speed whistle. Each locomotive had two, one for ordinary use and the other used as a powerful warning. To hear this most banshee-like sound coming down-wind even when three or four miles away had a special, eerie quality - now alas seldom heard. It is said that when the *King George V* made her visit to America the sound of this whistle brought tears to the eyes of expatriates from England who had gathered to see her go by. Even my dear late wife, who was no great train lover, used to say that one of the things she missed most on her long drives after the introduction of diesels was the beckoning column of smoke which every now and then appeared over the trees or round the side of a hill - a very evocative thing, a steam locomotive, however much they bore you.

Lucy on the Grand Union.

We continued on to Braunston Junction, at which point the Oxford turns right and the Grand Union comes in from the left. The junction is almost like that of a motorway, with a great triangle of an island in the middle with a magnificent iron bridge carrying the towpath. The length of the canal that we were on, whilst still nominally the Oxford, was part of the Grand Union main line, and the Grand Union Company was responsible for its modernisation and maintenance. That part of the canal from here to Napton Junction where the old Warwick and Napton section of the Grand Union takes over again was to have been modernised with the rest of the Grand Union, but unfortunately this work was never put through. As a result, it is still bedevilled by the Oxford's problems, such as comparative narrowness and shallows, besides having very bad corners at Wolfhampcote and two more particularly bad ones under the A425 at Shuckburgh. We arrived at Napton Junction and saw above us on the hill side Napton Mill, one of the boatman's favourite and most evocative landmarks, and I must say as a comparative newcomer I also came under its spell. We tackled the Napton flight; and then as we were once more on a strange canal we tied up. We had done well; would that we had been able to maintain this performance of nearly 32 miles in a day - our daily average was now 16.

By the time we had got to the top of Napton we were in high spirits, in fact the higher we got the more our spirits rose. It was now level or downhill all the way to Oxford, 28 locks and 46 miles. We were not sure where we would be tying up the next day, we had simply decided to get on as far as we could.

Apart from the fact that the summit tunnel at Fenny Compton has been opened up, the Oxford Canal south of Napton is virtually as originally conceived by James Brindley. It is rather narrow in cross-section and shallower than the upper half. There have been minor changes in recent years, such as the opening of so-called marinas (what have they got to do with the sea?) but otherwise the canal is mainly as built, and as such has a quiet beauty of its own, a condition even more apparent in 1950 than it is now. The tunnel was opened up in 1868; it had a length of 1,200 yards. Such is tradition that the cutting is still called "The Tunnel".

The summit is eleven miles long and a very twisty length of canal it is, except for the straight of the old tunnel. Then at the top of Claydon Locks, in the parish of Claydon with Chuttercote, the fall to Oxford starts, with eight locks in two and three-quarter miles. These locks, like all the other locks with the exception of Hillmorton, which are in pairs, were narrow, single locks. The eighth lock was at Cropredy, mentioned in Temple Thurston's *Flower of Gloster*, where there is a pub called the *Red Lion* and surprisingly in this very small village, a Co-op shop which was almost on the canal. In the years before the war the Co-op bought up quite a number of small village shops, very often to prevent them from closing down when their owners died or left for one reason or another. Generally they used to carry on with the old local suppliers; anyhow I remember that this shop used to sell the most delicious smoked bacon (English too) I think I have ever tasted.

We moved on down to Banbury where, in spite of what I had been led to expect from reading *Narrow Boat*, we did not find the canal particularly attractive. This was admittedly partly because I was continually on the look-out for possible return loads in conjunction with this salt run. The only cargo that I could see that had any possibilities was baled scrap metal from a canal-side wharf to the south of the town. But, as usual with canalside wharves, there were no facilities for cargo handling. The only trade was to Banbury Wharf and consisted of coal for the Co-op Dairy carried by Joe Skinner, and tar for Cowburn and Cowpar of Manchester from Banbury Gas Works. The town seemed to be east and west of the canal rather than north and south, resulting in most of the industry that there was being some distance away from the canal; it was obvious that there would be very little hope of back loading. It did not take us long to be out of the town area.

The canal from here to Oxford ran through the gently falling Cherwell Valley. There were locks, but fairly widely spaced, 16 in 27 miles, but there were 60 or more bridges of several kinds, many of them lift bridges of the typical Oxford variety. These were comparatively easy to work when you got used to them, but they all took time, so our progress was not as fast as we had hoped. We tied up that night at Aynho Wharf, having covered close to 28 miles and 13 locks. This was encouraging, but I did not know that fate and the weather were about to take a hand in our trials and tribulations and cause us yet more serious delays. We set off again next morning with high hopes; In the early afternoon we came round a corner above Enslow Lock to find a pair of S. E. Barlows tied up. On board was Dick Littlemore, no less, a most accomplished and experienced boatman. It would be most unusual for a man like Dick to be tied up unless he had illness on board, so we wondered what was up. As we drew alongside he beckoned me to stop, so I put *Columba* astern and drew back level. Dick was not his usual cheery self. He explained that the River Cherwell, which runs into the canal below the lock, was in full flood. He added that it would be foolhardy, at the least, to go on, and that was why he was tied up. If Dick thought the going dangerous, then that was something not to be ignored; if we had tried to take the boat through in such conditions we should almost certainly have capsized.

The reason for the flooding was that James Brindley, when he designed the canal, was very conscious of the need to provide a plentiful water supply that would not fail. In the very early days before there were efficient steam pumps, this could only be done by resorting to such a manoeuvre as running the canal through a river, which is what he had decided to do here, or flooding a valley to provide a reservoir. The upper half of the canal above Banbury was supplied by a reservoir built in the Claydon area and a larger one near Byfield. The use of a river is quite satisfactory when the particular river used is not in flood, which was certainly not the case now. The water level was very much higher than normal, both above and below the top and bottom gates of the next lock (Baker's or Gibraltar Lock). In addition, water was running at seven to eight miles an hour, possibly more, for three-quarters of a mile up to the point where the canal left the river at Weir Lock. This was bad enough, but what made it really dangerous was the fact that on a bend two or three hundred yards below Baker's Lock the river was crossed by a skew railway bridge whose supports were piled, thus reducing the navigable width to less than the canal width, and also worsening the swirl and eddying of the waters. So we decided to take Dick's advice and tie up until conditions had eased. This was to prove one of our worst days, if not the worst, with only four and a half miles covered and four locks passed. We were wondering how long we would get stuck; was it a matter of hours or days? We could only pray that we would get one or two rainless days over the land that fed the Cherwell.

The next day was fine, and we could see that the water level was falling. In the afternoon, Dick, Tom and I took a walk down past the railway bridge to the next lock, about three-quarters of a mile downstream. The bridge seemed to be quite a serious obstacle. We could see that the skew and the piling together reduced the channel by about a quarter. The level, and consequently the rate of flow, had dropped considerably since Dick had last been to take a look; even so, I was grateful when Dick offered to take *Columba* through for me. But it was mid-morning of the following day before this was possible. Tom went off to make sure that the next lock was ready, because we would not be able to hang around with the river running as fast as it was. Our speed through the water would still be about normal, four miles an hour. What made it dangerous was that the speed of the river would be at least eight miles per hour, possibly as much as 12, so that our ground speed would be anything between 12 and 16 miles per hour. This might be increased even further by the venturi effect caused by the piling under the bridge. Another fact we had to consider was the very short entry from the river into the lock. Coming off the river at 16 miles per hour into still water, if we were not to hit the bottom gates with a resounding crash, we should have to put astern very rapidly. We could also help to avoid crashing by using the additional safeguard of a check-rope on a bollard on the lockside, another reason for putting Tom off.

We started off and went through the bridge at great speed, but thanks to Dick's handling, with no difficulty and then into the lock without too much trouble. I should have explained that Dick was going to Wolvercote Paper Mills on what is called the Duke's Cut. This was not Brindley's first canal, which also had that name, but a branch from the Oxford Canal built towards Blenheim, which ran quite close, and was so named after the Duke of Marlborough. This was a coal traffic carried by S. E. Barlow, and Samuel Barlow Coal Company and Joe Skinner, the latter with his horse-boat, *Friendship*.

The Duke's Cut was also a short-cut into the River Thames for craft going up river towards Lechlade and would save them going down into Oxford, with all its complications, reducing the journey by about six miles and two locks. This was a distinct advantage before the locks on the River Thames between Oxford and Lechlade were modernised. The first of these schemes was in 1894, when a large amount of money was spent on four of the eight navigation weirs. More work was done, again involving four locks, in 1904. In spite of this, I see from my 1928 *Bradshaw* that there were still at that time three navigation weirs in existence, so it was worth giving these a miss when it was possible.

I suspect that the obsolete state of the upper river was in no small measure due to the exceedingly cumbersome nature of the administration, which included participation by such strange and ill-assorted bodies as the Admiralty (two Admirals), the Board of Trade, Trinity House (one Admiral and a Captain) plus many others representing County Councils, ship owners, dock owners and wharfingers, but at no time does there seem to have been any representation accorded to the Thames and Severn Canal, the Wiltshire and Berkshire Canal, the Oxford Canal or the Grand Union Canal. An excellent description of working the navigation weirs on the upper Thames occurs in C. S. Forester's *Hornblower and the Atropos*. Indeed, the book described the working of the far more modern locks on the Thames and Severn Canal in which Hornblower took part. I think it could be said that the deficiencies on the River Thames contributed to failure of both the Thames and Severn and the Wilts and Berks Canals. However, it is pleasing to see that both canals are now being restored.

We now moved on down the Oxford. On the outskirts of the city and on the canal bank in the Summerton area was the Radiator Factory of the Morris Car Company, again surely a missed opportunity for back loading to Coventry. The raw materials used in the factories could well have been carried by canal. We eventually got to Isis Lock, Oxford, on the twelfth day, and we were very conscious of the fact that we were now five days late. We slept well that night, oblivious of the delays and hazards that we were to encounter on the morrow.

At the time that we did the salt run in 1950, there were two stations in Oxford, the Great Western Station and that of the London, Midland and Scottish Railway (prior to 1923, the London and North Western Railway). We were tied up above Isis or Louse Lock, and from here to Four Streams there was a short branch of the river called in *Bradshaw* "The Branch to the Oxford Canal" and numbered 87a2. Four Streams was where the main River Thames (or Isis as it is called here) was joined by a tributary of the Seacant Stream. Between Louse Lock and Four Streams was the Great Western Railway Bridge on the north side of Oxford Station, which presented no great difficulty as there was plenty of headroom. But before this we would come to a real problem, the swing bridge which carried the LMS line into the station. It was a low-level swing bridge, controlled by the signal box to the north of the station. The railway company had an undertaking that the bridge could be swung at any time that there were no movements of trains into or out of the station. Passenger trains were unlikely to cause many delays owing to their comparative infrequency, but as the coal sidings were between the station and the bridge, there was a fair amount of shunting and movement of loose engines; this could well hold us up.

Early the next morning I went to the signal box to find out when the bridge could be swung. I was told that it could not happen for at least two hours. The swinging had to be done by railway staff, because not only had the bridge to be swung, but it also had to be jacked up first in order for this to happen. I went back to *Columba* and went through the lock and lay in the stream below, where to our dismay we found that the stream was running quite fast. The plan now was to be ready for moving off immediately we saw the gang were ready to swing the bridge.

Dick Littlemore had told me about Four Streams. The total length in which we had to move was one furlong, so we had to be pretty slippy. Straight away after the bridge, we had a 90 degree left turn, then we were directly under a low footbridge over the river. This had a very low springing to a low arch and the river was not very wide at this point (not much wider than *Columba*'s length) and was also running very high. We came out from the railway bridge at full throttle (this was necessary in full flood to keep control). The secret of this kind of turn is to get a good half-way across before you start to turn, engine going full pelt, then put your helm hard over and let the river do the rest. It is hair-raising, but fun while it lasts. *Columba* responded beautifully and we were round and in the middle of the stream with the top of our cratch a good 12 feet below the centre of the bridge.

Osney Lock was just under quarter of a mile away and open and ready for us. We found a very pleasant lock-keeper, who must have thought us a little mad, but he was at the same time most helpful with advice and said he would ring the next lock and tell them we were coming. He also warned us about the artificial cut by the gasworks where the restricted channel increased the rate flow of the water, which in the flood conditions we were experiencing add to our problems.

This cut was in the rough form of a letter S. We got through without difficulty and this made us aware that our boating skills had improved. On reflection, I realised that it was now 15 months since I had started boating and four months since Jim had left. I knew that it was entirely on account of that Jim had taught me that I was able to cope with all the trials that had arisen so far, and I had cause once more to be feeling grateful to him.

Next we reached Iffley Lock, and I recall that we paid a toll of 1s 9d in each lock. I may be wrong, but it is certainly the figure I have in my head. The Iffley lock-keeper rang Sandford Lock for us, and also warned us of the weirs that we were approaching, but assured us that each one was clearly marked. There were no problems at Sandford Lock, where again everything was ready for us by the time we got there. We paid our toll and asked the lock-keeper to ring the next lock, Abingdon. Consternation! Abingdon Lock was not on the telephone. But, he said, there should be no difficulties because there was a straight of about three-quarters of a mile down to the lock, so the keeper would be sure to see us well in advance. He advised us to switch on our headlight as we approached and to sound our klaxon as we got closer, then all would be well.

I should, I think, at this point make clear one or two facts about *Columba* and the river. We were drawing about three feet six inches to three feet eight inches, at which draught we had about nine inches freeboard; not all that much. *Columba*'s weight was 15 tons and our cargo was 20, so we had a total of 35 tons, which presented no problems on a canal, but we had no idea how this would handle in the swiftly flowing river. As I have said, we needed to be under full throttle for control and the river was in flood, about two feet deeper than the usual summer depth of three feet six inches, and running at some six miles per hour.

Looking along *Columba*'s cabin top

We did not even know if we could stop her if necessary.

The countryside for the next four miles to Abingdon was rather flatter than the previous four miles; this, combined with the extra height of water, meant that we could see for some miles distance ahead of us. As soon as we were through Nuneham railway viaduct, we could see Abingdon Lock about a quarter of a mile away, a distance we should cover in less than five minutes. It was clear that the lock was not ready for us and we could see no sign of the lock-keeper. It was about one o'clock and it occurred to us that he might be having his dinner, perhaps even in the local pub. We turned on our headlights to try to attract his attention, and stood ready to sound our klaxon, but still no lock-keeper appeared. Ahead and to the right was a very long weir and there was piling between the entrance to the lock and ahead the weir.

By this time *Columba* was being pulled slowly but inexorably broadside on. If we lay alongside the piles, would they hold and prevent our being carried over the weir? If the piles could withstand the pressure, could we find enough power in our engines to move off against the current once the top gates were opened? If we held there, would the water build up on our port side and flood the boat. These and other unanswered questions were filling my head when suddenly the lock-keeper appeared and began to fill the lock. By this time we were only about 150 feet from the weir and we were juggling with the tiller, the throttle and the river to try to keep *Columba* from her sideways drift towards it. At last the top gates were opened. During this time *Columba* had been pulling slowly ahead from the weir, every foot gained lessened the pull and thus imperceptibly increased our speed. Finally, we seemed to be clear of the river, but at right angles to the lock entrance. However, I did not judge it safe to reduce our speed, so that we hit the coping of the lock at around five miles per hour, which resulted in *Columba* rolling dangerously and at the time causing a pronounced ripple along her length. Then, miraculously it seemed, we were safely in still waters and inside the lock. It had been touch and go and we hoped that this was the last of our adventures. More were to come, however.

The three-inch V-shaped nick in the coping stone of the lock where our cast steel stem had hit it seemed to go unnoticed by the lock-keeper, who had been having his dinner when we approached. We waved him goodbye, shot Abingdon Bridge and passed what had once been the entrance to the ill-fated Wilts and Berks Canal, finally closed in the late twenties. It had been semi-derelict since about 1870, but still received a mention in the 1928 *Bradshaw*. It had never paid a dividend, and finished life with a boom from carrying building material for the Great Western Railway which paralleled it for the major part of its length. The GWR had built a station and goods yard wherever the canal had had a wharf.

The next lock at Culham was an easy one, like Clifton, Day's, Benson, Cleeve, Goring and Whitchurch, all of which had long cuts, so that we would be doing exactly what we had planned, namely to tie up above Mapledurham Lock. This we did just as it was getting dusk. Going through these other locks I reflected that the main trouble with Abingdon was not so much the weir, as the fact that there was no lock cut as with most of the other Thames locks. Thus, even in times when there was no flood, there was nowhere to go if the lock was not ready. A telephone was therefore a must at all times of the year and I hope that the Thames Conservancy have remedied the situation by the simple action of installing a telephone where it is really needed.

What a difference decent water meant! In spite of all our troubles, we had come 34 miles that day. We were now four and a quarter miles from Reading and 22¼ miles from Newbury, with only one river lock, and 22 on the Kennet and Avon Canal. Surely Newbury the following night was not too much to expect?

We made a leisurely start the next morning, cleared Caversham Lock, after a beautiful run down through Pangbourne and Goring from Mapledurham. I also remember that it began as a lovely sunny day, although it became somewhat overcast later. Then we came to the sharp turn into the Kennet and Avon Canal. The first mile was in fact the River Kennet section, and included Blake's Lock, which was controlled by the Thames Conservancy Board. The Kennet and Avon as such did not begin until High Bridge, Reading. So, goodbye to our friends on the Thames Conservancy and hello to men of the Docks and Inland Waterways Executive, who had turned out in force and were to prove most helpful.

Because of all the rain, the Kennet was running pretty fast; the normal rate of summer flow was three-quarters of a mile per hour - the

Unloading salt at Newbury from *Columba*

speed as we came to the canal was probably around four to six miles per hour. Bridge Street Bridge should have had headroom of about nine to ten feet, but this had been very considerably reduced by strengthening girders placed under it. Under normal conditions this would have given us headroom of about five feet six inches, ample for *Columba* to get under. Due to the flood, headroom was nearer four feet six inches or even four feet four inches. We required four feet eight inches as a minimum. We came very close to the bridge, and it was obvious that we were not going to get through by about eight inches and that was even after removing all the extras - mast, cabin ventilator, funnel, pigeon box, water can, chimney and so forth. Up to this time I had not considered all these items. By now I had tied up to the piling of the Tramway Depot so that we could have a think and something to eat. I decided that if the water level was lowered by opening the sluices at Blake's Lock and lowering any weirs above High Bridge, that we should probably be able to get under. This was done, and we had about 18 inches clearance under the bridge, but the lowering of the water had also increased the rate of flow. The extra pressure on *Columba* resulted in our pulling away the piling to which we were tied, and we had to save the situation by getting full power on the engine. So there we were, engine full ahead, and the water past us in the opposite direction at such a speed that we simply stayed still. The only solution was to ask them to reduce also the flow by partly closing the paddles of Blake's Lock, which would also raise the water level slightly. We cleared away all obstructions, my last action being to remove the brass knob securing the tiller. It was now a race as to whether we could get through before the water level grew high enough to jam us under the bridge. We were lucky and got under with a few inches to spare. Looking back almost immediately I could see that we had made it in the nick of time - already the water under the bridge was too high to give us sufficient headroom to pass. It had been a very near thing.

After this we went on to County Lock, where we paused both to get our breath back and to straighten the boat. Looking back after 35 years, I wonder at the foolhardiness of it all, particularly as it had been more cold-blooded than the risks at Enslow and Abingdon. But my blood was up, as we had nearly 22 miles to go to complete the journey. We had surmounted all other problems, alarms and excursions and I was blowed if I was going to be thwarted at this late stage, but, as sure as God made little apples, we could so easily have got jammed under that bridge, been pressed down as the water came up and have sunk.

So we were not sorry to see the last of Reading, and then two locks later, at Burghfield

Lock, we were regaled with the strange sight of a Harvey-Taylor coming towards us. It was John Gould in his motor boat *Colin* which, with her butty *Iris* he had bought from A. Harvey-Taylor of Aylesbury; actually he bought six boats, of which more anon. We were very pleased to see John, as *Colin* was a good boat with a good engine (a Russell Newbery) which could prove very useful in an emergency; a situation which was to come upon us later that day.

The canal above Burghfield Lock was very much silted up, because of a scour across the lock cut by the river and we were very glad to have *Colin* there to give us a snatch. We got very badly stuck downstream of Towney Lock, so I asked *Colin* to come alongside so that we could lighten *Columba*. *Colin* took about four tons of salt; fortunately they had top cloths, so that the salt could be sheeted up, and the boat was dry. We then went on until we got to Aldermaston, where we tied up for the night. John went back home for the night to Newbury, which was only about 10 miles away. We had agreed that I would leave first thing next morning and he would come back to *Colin* as early as he could. He was taken home by John Lester, who also brought him back again in the morning. We eventually arrived at Newbury with *Colin* at two o'clock on Friday, 24th February, and tied up at Newbury Wharf.

We started to unload into two lorries the next morning, using sack trucks and *Columba*'s slack boards as a bridge from the boat to the bank. We were very close alongside. The lorries belonged to Newbury Laundry and John Gould's sister Ruth, who had a haulage business. Tom made friends with several of the local lads who had come down to the wharf to see what it was all about. We finished the first part of the unloading at midday. I then

Unloading salt for Newbury Laundry at West Mills, Newbury, on the Kennet & Avon Canal.

went up to London to attend a Council Meeting of the Inland Waterways Association. Nothing happened the next day, Sunday, except that we began squaring up the boat. We recommenced discharging again the following day and finished about midday. I actually stayed in Newbury until the following Friday, March 3rd, mainly because one of the local lads, Bob Pettifer, had been recruited by Tom to come and work with us; he was to join us in a week's time.

We left Newbury that Friday morning at nine o'clock, arriving at Sheffield Lock, Theale at six o'clock that evening. On the way down to Theale when we got to Aldermaston, where we had tied up on the way down, we found a small pontoon bridge across the channel, which we assumed was an unauthorised obstruction, so we untied it at one end and left it floating loose. We set off for Padfield and when we got there we found a police car waiting for us. They wanted to know why we had cut the bridge adrift. This had been reported to them by Stirling Cables, who owned the factory at Aldermaston and had erected the bridge for the benefit of some of their staff who lived on the other side of the canal. I explained to the police that it had not been there when we came up on the previous Friday, John Gould had not seen it, and the D & IWE had not mentioned it either. As far as we were concerned, it was an unauthorised obstruction to navigation. The police were apparently convinced that we had done the correct thing.

As we went on down to Reading and the end of the first salt trip, we anticipated that we should be back with the next load in about three month's time. In actual fact it was to prove much longer. I thought that on the next trip we might be able to bring *Uranus* with us now that we were to have Bob. We now pressed on, back up the Thames to Oxford, and from there made very good time to Braunston, where we picked up *Uranus* once more.

Chapter Seven

LEARNING THE ROPES

We had left Bob behind so that he could get his gear together, wind up his job at Toomer's ironmongery (he had been a bicycle delivery boy) and say goodbye to his grandmother with whom he lived. We were to pick him up on the Oxford Canal at Fenny Compton at about five o'clock three days later. "How would he get to Fenny Compton?" you will say. Well, in those high and far-off times, those halcyon days, you could get a train at Newbury (a train that consisted of about three coaches pulled by a Great Western "Mogul"), which wound its way up over the chalk down to Didcot. Here a change was made and you took another local train through to Oxford and Banbury to Fenny Compton, probably in all a journey of about three-and-a-half to four hours.

On certain days there was a remarkable train which started in Southampton. Readers who are not particularly interested in railway operation must bear with me. The details of the train read like something from another world, a world we have lost and will never see again and which, I suppose, is the main theme of this book. This train started as the 07.33 from Southampton Terminus, calling via Winchester and all stations as far as Banbury. The reason that I use the word remarkable about it was that, in spite of this slow start, it then continued as a through train to York, Newcastle, Edinburgh and Glasgow. It conveyed a restaurant car from Oxford, which it reached at 15.18, and a through carriage to Scarborough on Saturdays only. As it finished up in Glasgow Queen Street (High Level) it presumably took the Great Central line from Banbury, with whom the Great Western had a very close working relationship. This was a truly extraordinary journey for a train which had started as an all-station train running over what used to be known as the Didcot, Newbury and Southampton Line. The Great Central main line, scrapped under the Beeching regime was, incidentally, the only main line in the country (apart from sections of the original broad gauge GWR) which was built to a continental loading gauge.

To return to our main story. We picked up Bob at Marston Doles on the Oxford summit, just a short distance from Fenny Compton Station. Actually we were an hour or more late, which caused Bob to be anxious about his supper. Coming up the Thames had not been the plain sailing for which we had hoped. The Thames still had a lot of water coming down, this time against us, and we had further delays on the Oxford Canal when we got to the Cherwell. We also had to stop and shop, which we did at Cropredy rather than Banbury, where the shops are some distance from the canal in the town.

By the time we reached Bob, as it was still March, he was not only anxious but also cold and hungry. As it was dark by then, we stopped on the summit until morning. In any case, Napton locked up for the night so there was nothing to be gained by going on. We should get to Braunston before mid-day the next day and spend the afternoon getting *Uranus* ready to leave early the next morning.

Now that Bob had joined us, it was important that he should "learn the ropes" as quickly as possible. Tom and I were experienced, so teaching Bob did not present much of a problem; practical demonstration was the quickest and easiest way to do this teaching. As the Chinese proverb says, "I do - I understand."

The first lesson proved to be a single lock, going uphill.

"Bob, the lock is ready for us, so here is what we do. Take the boat into the tail of the lock, leaving it in gear, just ticking over. Then hop off, let the boat go into the lock unmanned, then lift the top paddles to control the speed of the boat. When she is in, close the bottom gate and drop the paddles. Then go up to the top of the lock and lift all the paddles. When the lock is full, the boat will push the top gates open, so then be nippy. Close the top paddles, jump on to the boat and take her out of the lock. Do you get it?"

"I think so, Skipper".

"We'll see how you get on. I shall be here to keep an eye on you."

"What about Tom?"

"Oh, don't worry about him. He'll be going up the canal on the bike to get the next lock ready for us when we arrive."

I need not have worried. Bob picked it up very quickly and at the next lock was able to take the boat through single-handed without any help or advice from me. Then he asked,

"This is fine when the locks are ready. What happens if a lock is against us when we get to it?"

"It's no more difficult, just takes a few minutes longer. As you have already done, you leave the engine ticking over in the tail of the lock, then raise the bottom paddles and when the lock is empty the boat will push the gates open and slowly move in. The rest is just as before."

"Yes, I've got that, Skipper. It's quite straight-forward really, isn't it?"

I was very conscious of Bob's Berkshire burr. When we were past the summit level at Fenny Compton and approaching the first lock downhill, came Bob's next lesson.

"Skip, how do we go on here?" Bob asked.

"What you've got to look out for going downhill is getting the boat caught on the sill as the lock empties," I replied. "So, if the lock is ready, take her in, again leaving the engine just ticking over. Next, take a line off the stern and secure it round a bollard at the head of the lock to stop the boat moving backwards as the lock empties. Then, open the paddles and, when the lock is empty, untie the line and jump down to the cabin top ready to take over. Then Tom or myself will open the gates and jump onto the gunwale as you leave the lock."

Bob picked up this procedure very quickly and before long he was quite proficient. Then he came up with another question.

"What would be the quickest way of doing all this single-handed."

"That's fairly simple. Just wait as before until the lock is empty, then before jumping down on to the cabin top, open the gates and untie, so that the boat will move out slowly. You have the choice then; either jump down on to the cabin while she's in the lock and take her out, or allow her to move out and jump on at the tail of the lock. It all depends on circumstances."

After the nine locks downhill, we were into the Grand Union where Bob would have to learn how to cope with the wide locks and, once we had picked up *Uranus*, with the task of working through with both a motor and a butty. We reached Braunston in good time, as we were three-handed with a single craft. Now we would see how we would fare with both boats.

First, I explained to Bob the two ways of towing the butty. One was to breast up the butty alongside the motor and to secure it fore and aft, so we were like a double-hulled boat. He could see how this slowed down the speed of the pair. So then I said,

"We can also tow using two short straps."

"What are two short straps?" was the obvious question, and he asked it.

"These hemp ropes", I replied. "You see, they are about six feet long, about an inch in diameter and they have a spliced eye at each end." I put them both over the fore-stud of *Uranus*, letting one hang on either side of the bow. "This is where they are usually kept," I continued. "Now, I'll show you how to attach them to the motor."

I shouted to Tom and told him to back *Columba* under the butty's bows, then gave him the port strap, which he slipped over the starboard stud on *Columba's* counter, making sure it went under the bow. Then, putting *Columba* into forward, he took the starboard strap, took it under the bow and placed it on the port stud.

"There, you see, with the straps crossed like that, the butty will follow *Columba* without any trouble."

Just after Napton Junction comes the first lock downhill. Bob was keen to know how the procedure was going to differ with two boats to handle.

Descending Braunston top lock.

"The important thing to remember before we go through any of the locks," I told him, "is to remove the tiller handle of the butty and place it on the cabin top. If you don't, there is the strong likelihood of it swinging over in the lock and breaking off against the lockside."

"Right, Skip, I'll remember. I don't want my wages docked to pay for damages like that. Then what?"

The view from below Braunston top lock.

when you've got small children on board."

"I see. What size is the line?"

"It's about a hundred feet long and about half an inch in diameter. These cotton ropes can be very hard and abrasive when they're wet and stretched tight. They're what's caused those rub marks on the sides of bridges."

"Then we breast up the boats," I replied, "and go through exactly as we did with single locks.

"No problem then," Bob answered.

Travelling long pounds on the Grand Union, Bob was obviously keeping his eyes about him. Whilst we were eating, he asked me about what he had noticed.

"We're using two short straps for towing, aren't we? I've spotted that some of the pairs passing us aren't doing that. And they weren't all using the same methods as each other. Why is that?"

"Well, Bob, different methods for different circumstances. See, just approaching now, there's a loaded family pair. D'you see how they're towing? There's a long cotton line running from the stern of the motor, through a running block at the top of the mast and blocks along the top planks. It goes to a T-stud fitted into a socket at the fore-end of the butty hatch. The principle is that the line is wound round the T-stud to secure it, then it can be shortened or lengthened at will by the steerer of the butty. This is a safe method

"Oh, yes, I've often seen them on the bridges on the Kennet and Avon. Some of them are quite deep grooves too. So, they use a different method when it's not a family boat then?"

"Yes, then it's more usual for the boatmen to use a two-inch, seventy foot long coconut rope (snubber) with a spliced eye at each end. When working on long pounds, one goes over the port side near stud of the motor and the other over the fore-stud of the butty. Then, if the motor boat slows, slacking the line, the steerer of the butty shortens the rope. If the motor is going to slow down for a long while, then the steerer of the butty runs along the top planks, takes in the slack and resecures the line on the fore-stud."

"Runs along the top planks?" Bob seemed surprised.

"Oh yes, you soon get used to doing it. This way isn't used unless it's essential, because the coconut rope is very abrasive - much worse than the cotton line - and it's also bulky for coiling on the fore end."

"Yes, I can imagine so. So that's the

different ways of towing, then?"

"Not quite," I replied. "There's a third way, which is to use a hemp snubber. And, before you ask, that's about an inch in diameter and thirty to forty feet long - and like the coconut line it has a spliced eye at each end and is fixed in the same way. It's usually for short pounds or between locks. And all three of these methods are only used with loaded boats, of course."

"Whew, Skip, that's quite a bit. I think that's enough for now."

"Yes. Finish off that mug of tea and then go and take over from Tom or, better still, take the tea with you."

Kenelm leaving Braunston top lock, with Ron Wilson steering and Charlie Lane on gunwale.

Of course, when we arrived in Braunston, everybody wanted to know what we had been up to. One such was Ike Merchant. When he was younger, Ike used to work for Fellows, Morton and Clayton, and had worked the Oxford road. He had also been Captain of an FMC steamer when he was quite young, which would have been about 30 or 40 years earlier. He was now ashore, and the Samuel Barlow Coal Company had given him his own workshop where he made all the cloths for the company, looked after supplies of ropes and made their boats' bow and stern fenders and tip cats. He was quite short and the years had treated him well, even if he had to let out his broad leather boatman's belt. He used to wear a collarless shirt, white corduroy trousers, moleskin waistcoat and a black cap. He also had a walrus moustache and smoked a short pipe. I always found him to be a very good friend, very much his own man and a superb craftsman.

There were of course many others at Braunston who were of interest, and some of them will be mentioned when we come round to the building of *Lucy*. Meanwhile, we had a pair of boats to get ready for the northern road with a partially new crew. We had hoped to start the following day but it turned out that there were several more minor jobs to be carried out even on *Columba* after the adventures on the Thames and Kennet, so it was decided to postpone our departure for a further day.

So, two days after our arrival, and fuelled and provisioned, we set off from Braunston. Both boys were at this time on board *Uranus*. It had been decided that Tom should continue in *Columba* and that Bob should take over *Uranus*. I recollect that I had no say in the matter; it was decided by Tom and Bob between themselves, So, while Bob continued to sort out his belongings, Tom brewed up the inevitable cup of tea. We had a vast aluminium teapot which I had obtained when I was buying up gear for the boats before I actually got them started. It came from Beatties in Wolverhampton. It was in fact a very good purchase, being shaped like a large bap. It was squat and stable and had two handles.

We were travelling with *Uranus* close up under *Columba's* counter on two short straps. One advantage of this formation was that the butty required little steering, except perhaps when occasionally going through low bridges. Another advantage was the fact that it was easy to get from one boat to the other. Simply by standing on *Columba's* tip cat, it was possible to get up on to the bow of *Uranus* and was very convenient for passing cups of tea or plates of food and also, of course, for changing crews. Then, by climbing round the cratch, you could get to and from the butty's stern by walking along the planks which, as the boats were empty, were just laid on the beams. Care had to be taken approaching an awkward bridge when on two short straps, in a high wind. It would then be necessary to remove the butty chimney and water cans and put them in the middle of the slide. Overhanging trees and branches could also be awkward in a blow. When running with the butty on two short straps, the butty tiller would be secured in the dead fore-and-aft position by the two, short, spliced loops attached to a fixing either side of the slide on the cabin top so that there was no movement and the butty, as explained earlier, simply followed the motor. To steer the butty, the two spliced loops were removed and the tiller used in the normal way. However, in most circumstances, the butty had to go where the motor went and, provided the steerer did not go to sleep, all would be well.

The tapered hole in the top of the helm, into which the tiller fitted, was inclined at an angle of about five to ten degrees out of the vertical. The tiller itself, which was also tapered to fit in the helm, was curved throughout its length so that at the end it was parallel to the top of the slide. When the boat was moored, the tiller was unshipped, turned over and put back into the helm again and, because of its shape, it stuck right up in the air so that it was possible to get in and out of the cabin without having to dodge the tiller.

John Knill steering butty *Uranus* in 1951.

I had, of course, been to Birmingham with Jim many times, but we had always been loaded; now we were empty and whilst some of the techniques for working the locks on the Birmingham road were similar, there were some differences. This road had been (before the formation of the Grand Union Canal Company) the Warwick and Napton and the Warwick and Birmingham Canals. There were, in all, 10 groups of locks on the old Warwick and Napton section, some in flights of from two to nine locks and a few single locks, some of which could be considered to be part of the flights. There was included in the flights one staircase of two. The old Warwick and Birmingham length had by far the more formidable obstacles; namely five at Knowle and 21 at Hatton, which constituted one of the longest flights in the country.

All these locks, on both sections, had been built by the same contractor, Ham, Baker and Company Ltd of Broadway, London, W1, at the time of the Grand Union modernisation scheme of the early thirties. All of them were built to replace the single locks of the old canals. As regards size, both in length and beam, they were the largest locks on the Grand Union and, for that matter, on most of the canals in the country with the exception of river navigations. They were also deeper over the sill than other locks on the Grand Union. The result of all this was to have been that the Grand Union could boast of having the most modern and easily-worked canal in the country. However, before the scheme could be fully implemented, the money ran out. The locks planned were all completed. Miles of canal were piled with steel and concrete, a certain amount of dredging was done, but many of the old accommodation bridges were left as they were, which presented difficulties when operating the larger boats of the new Grand Union Canal Carrying Company fleet, especially those of the large Town class built at Northwich and North Woolwich. The smaller Star class boats, which had less side but were also built at Northwich and North Woolwich, were not all that much larger in beam and side than the traditional boats; they were, however, bluffer and fuller in the bows and stern. The failure to improve the old bridges also killed another project. It was hoped that if all the modernisation plans had been carried out, it would have been possible to run wide boats all the way to Birmingham either from Regent's Canal Dock or Brentford, or even on to the Thames itself. Whilst narrow boats could and did successfully operate from the two former sites, they were not particularly satisfactory on the Thames itself when fully loaded because of their low freeboard, the low power of their engine (only eighteen horse-power for a pair) and the danger to crews operating on a comparatively rough and fast flowing river, particularly with an ebb.

So an experimental wide boat was built by Bushell's of Tring and named *Progress*. She was built of wood, was 72 feet long and 12 feet in beam and had a 30 horse-power diesel, probably a Russell Newbery. She was fitted with hatch covers, rather than side and top cloths, but was in all other respects similar to a narrow boat with after cabin and tiller, steering from the counter. It was hoped, in view of the double-sized cabin, that she would attract the family boatman and would in all respects be a slightly smaller version of the barges used on the Dutch and French canals at that time. However, when she was completed, there were grave operational problems owing to the lack of attention given to bridge holes and to bends during dredging, and she was never a success, eventually being used as a maintenance boat before being broken up *[she was not in fact broken up, and is currently being restored]*.

She had one brief moment of glory. She was used to convey the Royal Party for the opening of the new locks - H.R.H. Prince George, Duke of Kent, and the Board of Directors. The Grand Union Canal Carrying Company might have learnt from other great leaps forward. The "Great Bear" and "King" class locomotives of the GWR were all restricted operationally to certain routes because insufficient attention had been given to loading gauge requirements, the same as with Progress.

Ironically, it could be said that if the Grand Union Company had spent more on improving the canal and less on building a large carrying fleet, they, or their successors, could be in business today. The reasoning behind this proposition is that between the years 1930 and

Coming down Bascote staircase locks

1935, approximately 180 pairs of boats of many sizes were built, including small Woolwich, small Northwich, middle Northwich, large Woolwich and large Northwich, plus smaller numbers built by Walker Brothers of Rickmansworth and Bushell's of Tring; the former mainly large and small butties were built on the expectation of traffic which never materialised. For a number of years, the Wendover and Aylesbury arms and Widewater were full of brand-new or nearly-new motors and butties, slowing deteriorating. Large numbers were sold off (including *Columba* and *Uranus*) and as early as 1948 some had been converted into houseboats, as they were then called. Various subsidiary companies were formed to try to get additional cargoes, such as the Flixborough Shipping Company of Burton-on-Trent, from whom I purchased *Epsom* and *Dunstable* (to be renamed *Kenelm* and *Dunstan*). What I am saying, is that probably a fleet of half the size would have been sufficient and, with the money saved, greater improvements could have been made to the canal north of Napton Junction; probably more money could have been saved by reducing the number of narrow boats and building steel wide boats of the *Progress* type in lieu. This in due course would have overcome the manning problems because there may well have been less wastage of those crews who left because of inadequate schooling for their children. It would also have meant better living conditions because of the larger unified cabins and less arduous working conditions. A wider range of cargoes could have been carried because of the larger holds and the carrying capacity would still have been between 45 and 60 tons. There could have been better weather protection for the steerer, and the boats could have been used on the Thames and not been confined to the canals.

The only disadvantages that I can see is that sections of the canal would have had to be widened, but 40 feet on the Kennet and Avon was enough for two wide boats to pass, if the road was properly maintained as regards dredging and overhanging branches and so on. Boats would have had to assemble in trains when tunnels were encountered, but this was normal practice anyhow on narrow canals. No, the real disadvantage that I can see, is that *Columba* and *Uranus* might not have been sold, or even built, and this book not written.

It is interesting to record that Fellows, Morton and Clayton - the largest canal operators in the country - also considered the possibility of wide boats and built *Pioneer*, I believe at about the same time as *Progress*, to take full advantage of the new locks. I think that the tragedy of the Grand Union was that although the locks were wide, it remained in essence a narrow canal, at any rate from Berkhamsted northwards. Vokin's horse-drawn barges used to operate as far as that town.

Under post-war nationalisation, a scheme had been put forward for widening the canal as far as Cowroast, I believe, in an endeavour to help keep the lorry out of London. But it would have cost an astronomical amount of money. It is exhilarating to wonder - what if this decision had been taken in 1933?

In spite of all the foregoing, narrow boats would still have been necessary because of the many miles of canals in the south east of England which were operated with narrow locks. The wide boats would have been restricted to the Grand Union Canal proper, the River Lee, the Lee and Stort Navigation, the Rivers Thames, Wey and Kennet and the Kennet and Avon and Basingstoke Canals.

The Warwickshire coalfields, London's main source of coal supply, the Northampton and Aylesbury Arms, the Oxford and Leicester Cuts would all have been areas where the narrow boat was king because of the narrow locks. Perhaps this would have been no bad thing as it might have kept a lot of the true Number Ones and the smaller companies in business.

Enough of this daydreaming. We are now at Napton Junction, where we were to turn right into the old Warwick and Napton Canal for our first taste of these new locks, which were all downhill. Fortunately, the top lock happened to have been made ready by the last pair coming uphill. This gave some indication of the amount of trade on this canal, as we had not passed anybody since leaving Braunston and obviously there was at least one loaded pair ahead of us. The boats coming uphill must have crossed with the Brummagem bound pair below the top lock, otherwise more locks would have been ready. Probably the pair that had come up would have had orders for Coventry, Newdigate or Griff Collieries or they would have gone the bottom road.

Columba entering a Grand Union lock. Note the steamer style funnel, fitted to many GU motor boats when built in the 1930s.

So I undid one of the short straps so that *Uranus* would slide into the lock in her accustomed place to the left of the motor. Both boys had jumped off, closed the top gates and were about to get the paddles up but, before we could do this, we had to get the boats well breasted up. Whenever doing this for working through locks, it was always important to get the boats alongside each other as snug and tight as possible and for this we used the fore and aft cotton mooring lines which were quite strong enough and far easier to handle then hemp.

I was on the motor; Tom had gone on to get the next lock ready and Bob was winding up the paddles at the bottom of the lock. I gently eased the boats against the bottom gates with the engine so as not to get caught on the sill with one or even with both boats. These locks were usually quite simple to work, but could be dangerous if you opened the paddles too fast. The actual opening for each paddle was about three feet square and there were two top and two bottom. All four were ground paddles; there were no gate paddles. With openings of that size, if opened to the full, they could give your boat a virtually uncontrollable drop of up to 10 feet with consequent risk of damage.

Each paddle required 22 turns to get a full opening, so it was usual to start with about five or six turns, gradually increasing the total of turns up to the full 22, by which time the lock was practically empty.

When working uphill with a pair of loaded boats, whether you had side cloths up or not, you could easily ship so much water that the boat would sink. In addition to this, the turbulence could rock you so violently that it was possible for your gunwales to go under; the fore decks could be awash and water could be shipped through the cabin lid if it were not properly secured.

Bob by now had both gates opened; Tom had got the next lock ready and was opening the second of the top gates, so we were on our way. Tom had the bike, just in case, and was on his way to get the next lock ready. Bob had jumped on to the butty as she came out of the lock and so we went into the next lock, Bob on the fore end of the butty. He jumped off as we came into the lock, ran back and closed the butty's gate and I eased the motor and butty against the bottom gates, and then ran back and closed the motor's top gate, and we both checked that the paddles were properly down. Bob, meanwhile, had opened the bottom paddles. I was back on the motor and, at a signal from me, Bob raised the paddles some more. "By the time we get to the bottom of this flight", I thought to myself, "he should know what he's up to and be able to give Tom a spell from lock-wheeling."

We were now coming to the top of the Itchington flight and were passing the short cut to one of the many lime and cement works that abounded in this section of the canal, such as C. Nelson and Company Ltd. of Stockton; Gleaves; Bull and Lakin; and Kage and Company Ltd. At one time, The Grand Union Canal Carrying Company, and later the Docks and Inland Waterways Executive, had a fair traffic from here down to the Rugby Cement Company in Warwick for several pairs of boats each week, month in and month out. It was not a very popular traffic with the boatmen as it was something of a treadmill. It was perhaps not too bad in decent weather but when it was damp or wet it was very unpleasant. Even in fine weather, the boats had to be sheeted up to protect the cargo and, of course, in wet weather there were problems in loading and unloading.

The run was not particularly long, only about 11 miles to Nelson's Wharf through Leamington. There were about 18 locks to be worked and, owing to the need to be breasted up all the time, progress was slower than it would normally have been, except through Leamington itself when the boats could be singled out. The nature of this work meant that most of the working time was taken up with loading, sheeting up side and top cloths, washing down the boat after loading, unsheeting, unloading, washing down again and sheeting up once more to travel back uphill empty (particularly essential in wet weather). And so it went on, round and round. Each pair was generally only expected to work short spells on this run but, even so, it was hard work and usually went to pairs with large crews.

There were 27 locks between Napton and Budbrooke, all but two of which were downhill. We were now negotiating the short pound at the bottom of Radford Locks. The greater part of this, which was about five miles long, passed through what was then the commercial part of Leamington Spa. I was very careful to choose the word "negotiate", because that was what the condition of the canal required. Most of the pound was exceedingly shallow so that with a good load on - say, 50 to 55 tons - you were running in water, it is true, but water so foul that it seemed unbelievable that a town with the reputation and standing of Leamington Spa should allow such foulness within its boundaries. One might think one was running in three feet six inches of water but at least one foot of this was liquid mud and woe betide any boatman who had the misfortune to get anything around his propeller in all this filth. We had done this on two previous occasions. The first was the remains of a spring mattress and the second a coil of rusted barbed wire. Fortunately, on this trip with the two boys we were lucky, as we were travelling light and picked up little that caused any trouble.

We were now approaching Cape Locks. By this time, I think, Healey with his sports car factory (almost in the early days a back-yard industry) had left the area for pastures new and more commodious. There was a pub here called *The Cape* which stood almost on the side of the Cape Locks. Here we decided to tie up for the night.

The following morning we moved off, soon passing Budbrooke where the old Warwick and Napton Canal joins the Warwick and Birmingham, which does not stop here but runs for another half a mile to form Warwick Wharf, roughly in the centre of the town. There is a wharf here called Timber Crane Wharf, presumably because there was here a timber crane of the sort that appears not only on many canal prints but also in early railway pictures. There is, to this day, a very fine example of such a crane on Great Bedwyn Wharf on the Kennet and Avon, which I saw in 1948 when I cycled along the canal.

Jim Jackson on *Columba* on the Grand Union Canal at Brentford, June 1949. Photo: Jack Gashion

About a quarter of a mile after leaving Budbrooke, we came to the bottom of Hatton flight to find the locks against us. We had been singled up again since leaving the Cape so, cutting the propeller, we got the butty alongside and breasted up with the bows against the bottom gates. I put the engine in gear and going slow, then we all three went up on to the lock by the steps provided. I took with me a strap which was attached to the back end rail of *Columba*. Both boys raised the bottom paddles by about eight turns so as not to cause too much turbulence under the boats. It was well not to forget those three feet square paddles, needing to be that size to allow the speedy filling of the chamber which, like all these new locks, had a capacity of seventy-five thousand gallons of water. These had to fill quickly so as not to slow down the speed of the boats through the locks, about five minutes per lock. The new locks in the Hatton and Knowle flights were alongside and roughly at the same elevation as the old single locks. The obvious reason for this method was that the single locks could continue in operation, switching to the new ones as each was completed.

This gave rise to a statement in the *National Geographic* magazine in 1940 that the new ones had been built alongside the old ones as a precaution in the event of bombing! What naivety on the part of the *National Geographic* Editor, not only to think that a mere 15 or 20 feet would have been any real protection, but also that a British Government could have been so forward-looking in 1933!

The lock was now empty; the boys had opened the bottom gates; the boats moved gently in and were checked short of the sill by the strap already mentioned, using one of the stumps provided for this purpose. The paddles were wound down (they had to be wound, not dropped), the ground paddles were eased up a few turns and the gates closed. When the lock was about half full, the paddles were wound up to the top of their travel and secured. There were no ratchets on these paddles, instead there was a kind of square plate on a chain. In the plate there was a square notch which was put over the winding spigot when the windlass could be taken off. The locks filled quickly; the top gates were pushed open by the boats and we moved out into the pound. The boys had already gone ahead to repeat the process on the next lock which is some little distance away. We remained breasted up and I steered the two boats up to the next lock and so on to the top of the flight of 21, the third equal longest flight in the country.

We took about two hours to get to the summit, which was comparatively slow for empty boats, as a loaded two or three-handed pair had been known to do it on many occasions in as little as one and a half hours. My shortest time two-handed was with Jim, as far as I can remember, one hour and fifty minutes. Hatton flight was paralleled all the way to the top by the Great Western Railway main line. This is now reduced to a branch line *[it was later reinstated, as the Chiltern main line from Birmingham Snow Hill to London Marylebone]* but, up to the end of steam in 1963, the spectacle from the boats was truly magnificent. The incline was one in one hundred and to see and hear a double-chimneyed "King" thundering up Hatton is something that had to be seen and heard to be believed. I have a magnificent recording of *King Richard III* climbing Hatton with a 15 coach train and never at less than 50 miles an hour. Such is the clarity of the sound that you can actually hear the train as it leaves Leamington Spa and the notes of a blackbird singing, the latter being gradually obscured by the blast and roar of the train. As the train clears the summit, you hear the clang of the signal arm rising, then the sound of the train disappears into the distance and gradually there is audible, once more, the song of the blackbird.

Halfway up Hatton flight there used to be a lunatic asylum, and there is a story of some of the inmates sitting on top of the wall roaring with laughter at the antics of the boatmen working their way up through the locks and telling them they ought to be inside with them!

We got to the top, singled up and set off for the next flight of five at Knowle, where the drill was repeated. However, before we got to Knowle, there was Shrewley Tunnel to be negotiated, quite a short tunnel, only 433 yards long, but a foot wider than Blisworth Tunnel at 16 feet and about two feet higher above the canal.

After Shrewley, we passed Kingswood Junction and the entrance to the Stratford-upon-Avon Canal, the bottom part of which was soon to be handed over to the National Trust, one of the early campaigning successes of the IWA. Once the trade had gone from the southern section, very little revenue was received, except for the odd pleasure craft that fought its way through the dereliction. With the demise of the Upper Avon Navigation, the canal really led nowhere. There was also no access to the Avon, as the Stratford Town Council had lowered the bridge at the bottom end, thus effectively cutting off any exit. However, within 10 years or so, this was all to be remedied and the canal reopened by the Queen Mother. Also, locks and sluices were rebuilt to reopen the Upper Avon. It is still hoped eventually to connect up with the Grand Union at Warwick thereby opening the Higher Avon to traffic.

The northern end of the Stratford-upon-Avon Canal was a different matter as it was a through route (even if not often used) from the Grand Union at Lapworth to the Worcester and Birmingham Canal at Kings Norton Junction, thus also giving access to the southern part of. the Birmingham Canal Navigations.

My own feelings are not so much wonder that the Birmingham canal system was remarkable for having, as we are very often told, more miles of canal than Venice but rather that it should have any canals at all, when it is realised that to make possible this extensive amount (148 miles) it was necessary to build between 250 and 300 locks. If Rome achieved fame for being built on seven hills, how much greater should the fame of Birmingham be for being built on 40! If you also remember that the building and engineering arts had not changed very much in the two thousand years between the two eras, it becomes a truly remarkable achievement.

Basically, the Birmingham system was arrived at by building on three levels. The first was the original level of Brindley and Smeaton, to be followed by Telford's short cuts and improvements by the provision of massive embankments and cuttings, which rendered much of the original work redundant, but which was kept to facilitate trade, and then the final improvements which followed on after Telford.

The Birmingham Canals in those days when we passed through with *Columba* and *Uranus* were teeming with commercial craft of all types and with all kinds of cargoes, including narrow boats carrying coal and manufactured goods and many other freights. There were Clayton boats, Cowburn and Cowpars, tankers carrying tar and gas-oil, and masses of day boats pulled both by horses and by diesel tugs. Tugs could be old motor boats, generally of wood, and some were owned by Ernie Thomas and by Element. A day boat was a boat without a cabin of any sort or, in some cases, a minimal cabin in which the steerer could huddle from the weather when he had a chance. This cabin included a very basic heating stove, on which he could cook what was also an equally basic meal. The boats without cabins were often used as rubbish boats by the Corporation of the City of Birmingham.

When full, they could be towed to the rubbish wharves and dumps and the cargoes craned out. Many of these boats were owned by Ernie Thomas and Element, as well as by the City of Birmingham. It was possible to come across nests of these rubbish boats filled with every conceivable kind of material from rubble to dredgings and steel scrap. They used to lie outside factories and alongside wharves until tugs or horses arrived to take them away.

All around them the surface of the canal and towpath were covered in dust, slime and oil. Now, most of this trade, which must have seemed haphazard and unrewarding, has gone. I say "seemed", because the charges and tolls imposed by the Birmingham Canal Navigations on these craft must have been the backbone of canal funds to pay for the upkeep of the Navigation.

Where there were no locks (such as on the Wolverhampton levels, which ran from Wolverhampton at least as far as Tipton, a distance of some six miles on the main line without including all the various arms and loops of the old system), some craft were not restricted to the 72 feet by 7 feet dimensions of the normal narrow boat. This latitude in size was generally applied to length rather than beam because of the various gauging stations through which the boats were expected to pass. These consisted on narrow sections of up to seven feet six inches width and having either no gates or single gates for staunching off sections of the canals for repairs, but with no restriction on length. Gauging stations were often on an island site in the middle of the cut, with a small office for the clerk and a simple plank bridge.

Gauging was the method used to check the tonnage carried by working boats Jon the canals. The method was to measure the amount of freeboard a boat had, in two places, one aft and one near the stern. By checking this measurement against a set of tables giving how much freeboard there should be for various amounts in tons of cargo, the weight carried could be calculated. It was, in fact, a practical use of the famous Theory of Archimedes. On the Grand Union there were gauging stations at Cowley, Cowroast, Tring Summit, Stoke, Buckby, Braunston, Hillmorton and Hawkesbury Stop.

There were many tunnels on the Birmingham system, ranging from the minimum size possible to the gigantic. Of the former, the one on Dudley No. 1 Line was probably the smallest, Dudley Tunnel: length 3,127 yards, minimum height five feet nine inches, minimum width eight feet five inches, too small for ordinary narrow boats and suitable only for day boats with their smaller cabins. All boats had to be legged through. This tunnel was still nominally open at the time of the publication of my 1928 *Bradshaw*. Another tunnel on the Dudley No. 2 Line was even worse, being 3,795 yards long, minimum height six feet, minimum width seven feet nine inches. This one had been closed by 1929.

In complete contrast was Netherton Tunnel, 3,027 yards long with a height of 15 feet 9 inches and a minimum width of 27 feet, including a towing path on each side and a water width of 17 feet. It was equipped with electric light before 1928. In 1904, it had been lit by gas.

The route we took after leaving the Grand Union was as follows. At Salford Junction with the Birmingham and Fazeley Canal for three and a quarter miles and 24 locks at Aston, all single and then to Tipton Factory, eight and a half miles and three locks (again, all narrow - in fact we were not to see any wide locks for many miles and months). We now had another five and a half miles to travel and then the top of Wolverhampton Locks and the flight of 21 downhill. By this time, we had the drill of working single locks with the butty off pat. We now had experience of the drill needed for both uphill and downhill flights. This included seven downhill at Bordesley, six on the Digbeth Branch of the BCN, all uphill, by the Aston flight already described.

Wolverhampton flight of 21 is a long, serpentine flight, starting almost in the centre of Wolverhampton with its rows of back-to-back houses and factories, all in those days pretty dingy after four and half years of war. Halfway down the flight, the landscape begins to open up, firstly with the engine sheds and yards of the old London, Midland and Scottish Railway, and then the Wolverhampton race course almost alongside the cut. As can be imagined, there were several tying-up places here. Then the final drop to Aldersley Junction, the junction with the Staffordshire and Worcestershire Canal. When we reached that point, since leaving Wolverhampton we had travelled just under one and a half miles and worked 21 locks - in canal terms almost a sheer drop.

We turned right at the junction and then a quarter of a mile further on we turned left on to the Shroppie - the Shropshire Union - on the Birmingham and Liverpool Junction Canal. Once again, I renewed my acquaintance with the toll clerk, Sam Lomas.

It was getting late by now, so we decided to tie up for the night, which we did just clear of the "stop place". After a good meal we turned in, for the next day would be a long one. We had already agreed to take advantage of the locking-up times on the Shroppie to run right through to Middlewich, a distance of 52 miles and 32 locks, but from the nature of the canal, easy to work. Great cuttings through the solid rock, all dead straight and just wide enough for two boats to pass, characterise this part of the canal.

There was much foliage, especially ivy, clinging to and growing out of the rock, which was mainly hidden, so that there was the impression of sailing through a dense jungle with complete or nearly complete silence, the engine having to run slow so as not to pull the counter down on to the bottom of the canal. Every now and again there would be a bridge, but what a bridge! They were probably 40 feet high to the crown of the arch, the road at the top flush with the cliff top. It would also be possible sometimes to get a glimpse of two bridges in a line and appreciate once more the skill of Thomas Telford.

Suddenly the cliff would disappear and your eyes had to get used to the broad sweep of the canal, twice as wide as heretofore, as it strode across the countryside on a vast embankment, pushing its way northwards across the Cheshire Plain, finally reaching Nantwich Basin, where the canal joined the former Chester Canal Navigation.

But do not think that the canal had been level for the last 39 miles. First of all, there was the lock at Wheaton Aston which gave the excuse for shopping at the Post Office whilst the boats were worked through. We had come seven and three-quarter miles

Kenelm loading timber.

since Autherley, then 18 miles and five locks to Tyrley, then four and a quarter miles to Adderley Top and one and a quarter miles to the 15 locks at Audlem, followed after four miles by two more locks at Hack Green. This was fairly heavy lockage - 28 locks in 36 miles - but so spaced and engineered that they were almost a pleasure to use. They had fine paddle gear, were beautifully maintained, and above all featured the wide vistas of Cheshire Plain and its wonderful skies.

Rarely did we see another pair; more often than not it was a single Josher, with an occasional pair of Cowburn and Cowpar horse-boats, spotlessly clean in spite of their cargo of gas oil or tar. At Nantwich there was a large canal basin. The warehouses around its edge have long been gone, but they used to be filled with Cheshire cheeses maturing or waiting shipment north and south.

Three and a half miles further on is Barbridge Junction and the Middlewich Branch of the Shropshire Union Canal. Picture if you will a large Victorian railway station with an overall roof; such was Barbridge Junction with its covered wharves for boats to discharge free from the weather, but even then a sadly deserted and crumbling relic of the great canal age. How I wish that I had taken photographs of these and other wonders when passing along the waterways, but somehow I do not think it occurred to me - and I am not sure if I even had a camera at that time. My best camera I lost when I was blown up in Aisha in 1940. It was not an expensive camera, but a novel one, designed by the great American designer, Loewe. It was called a Perma Special and had three speeds (1/40, 1/125 and 1/400 of a second). The speed was selected by cunning balance weights according to which way the camera was held.

So here we were at Minshull Lock and it was time for breakfast. Our night run had been fun and at times strangely eerie. Of course we had not all been on duty the whole time. We all turned out for locks, but with the butty on two short straps only one man was required most of the time. We then went on to Anderton. On our arrival at the beginning of the Trent and Mersey Canal, I telephoned to the Liverpool office of the D & IWE Northern Division and spoke to Mr C. S. Hall (Sales Manager). It was now Tuesday and we had to be in Manchester Docks to load on Friday morning.

Those two days gave us time to fuel and make things ready, and to leave on the second day. Our route was to be from Anderton to Waters Meeting. That is on along the Trent and Mersey to the junction with what was affectionately called the Duke's Cut, and through the three tunnels in the eight miles or so to Waters Meeting. Two of the tunnels were quite short, Barnton 572 yards and Saltersford 424 yards. By far the longest was the third, Preston Brook at 1,239 yards. All were reasonable in size, about 13 feet 6 inches wide, but too narrow to allow two boats to pass. In the old days, they used to make up a train of boats which were pulled through by the company's steam tugs. From 1923, the canal came under the London Midland and Scottish Railway Company, and after nationalisation, the D & IWE. The Duke's Cut at this time was part of the Manchester Ship Canal as, under the 1948 Act, Manchester Docks and its associated companies were not nationalised. These companies included the Bridgewater Canal and Manchester Liners (not part of the MSCC), alongside one of whose ships, *Manchester Trader*, we were to load our cargo of baled cotton wool which we would be taking to Stourport.

At Waters Meeting, we turned left on the Duke's Cut and we made a run of five miles to the top of Runcorn Locks - not the original 10 locks built when the canal was first opened, but the new flight of 11 which had superseded them. Through them, and we were down on the Manchester Ship Canal.

Normally narrow boats were not allowed to navigate the Ship Canal by themselves, so we had to pick up a tug to take us through to the actual Docks some 24 miles away. As far as I can remember, the *Manchester Trader* was a vessel of about 7,000 tons, and the pair of us would undoubtedly have the appearance of the proverbial flea and the elephant. We were to be alongside at about eleven in the morning, so having tied up next to the ship we got the boats ready and had a good meal, and turned in so as to be ready for the coming morning's work. Our cargo was to be 44 tons, and we decided that we should take about 20 tons in *Columba* and the remainder in *Uranus*. Fortunately, the weather was dry with little wind to ruffle the surface of the dock. Loading took about three and a half hours. The bales were big and heavy, so we had no trouble with *Columba's* short hold. Once the boats were loaded and sheeted up, we collected our chits and were away.

We would not be going back the way we had come, but through the Hulme Lock on the Bridgewater Canal. This was to prove as interesting in its way as our journey along the Ship Canal. However, our main regret was that we should not be going over that wonder of waterways, the Barton Swing Aqueduct.

On the continent of Europe, canals and waterways go from strength to strength, from the locks 70 feet deep in Northern Spain to the world-famous inclined plane at Ronquieres in Belgium (constructed as recently as 1968). Here in England, everything seems to have stopped in the concluding years of the last century. All the great works were completed by 1900 - Pontcysyllte Aqueduct in 1805, the Anderton Boat Lift in 1875, the Barton Swing Aqueduct in 1894 and the Foxton Inclined Plane in 1900. Over the years there have been numerous Royal Commissions which should have resulted in canal improvements and developments. However, the proposals made in most cases were that action should be taken to improve, modernise and encourage our inland waterways. But as usual, governments of all colours chose to ignore the proposals and do virtually nothing. I suppose the last occasion when any serious effort was made was the modernisation of the Grand Union Canal in 1934, an effort which because of government lethargy had burnt itself out by 1940. Nationalisation in 1948 put the canals at first under the Docks and Inland Waterways Executive - but nothing was done in the way of improvements. Then it became British Transport Commission's concern - still nothing - and now finally British Waterways does little, but too late and too limited in nature. Now, instead of a thriving system of working canals, as there should be, there is commercial operation over a few miles of canal in the north and sometimes on the Gloucester Sharpness Canal in the south-west. But once again neither government nor industry seems interested enough to develop the full potential of what is left.

However, to return to Brindley's wonder aqueduct at Barton over the River Irwell, this was demolished when the Ship Canal was built following the course of the river. The new aqueduct is composed of a swinging span 234 feet long and weighing 1,600 tons. There are electrically operated stop gates at both ends of the span and at the two canal ends. A wonder indeed! Now, even this is rumoured to be at the end of its useful life because of lack of government support for our greatest inland port which is virtually closed and being turned over to luxury apartments. Truly we are a strange race. But back in 1950, most things seemed to be rosy, and commercial carrying was an interesting and hopeful way of life.

We were now south-bound from Manchester along the Duke's Cut again with 44 tons of baled cotton for Stourport, via the Shroppie and the Staffordshire and Worcestershire and finally to the River Severn. The boys, Tom and Bob, were working well together and were handling the boats well.

By now I should have introduced the fourth member of the crew - Bosun – a Schipperke dog about two years old. He was a present from my grandmother and my mother, who had decided that a boat needed a dog, and what better than a Belgian barge dog. The breed is very small, very black, and in certain postures the creature looked a bit like the Lincoln imp. They are also very good watchdogs and reputedly very good ratters, although I have no actual proof of this. They are very affectionate to their friends, as Jim and Joe had found in the past, and Tom and Bob were discovering too. When I went lock-wheeling, Bosun used to follow me for miles without tiring.

As Bosun was a pedigree dog, I took him one day to a show of the Schipperke Club at the Wigmore Hall in London. I was rather disconcerted when everyone who saw him burst out laughing. Apparently all that lock-wheeling and hearty eating had developed him prodigiously, and he was now far too big to be considered for any sort of prize. His name had been my grandmother's choice. My grandfather, who was in the Merchant Navy at the turn of the *[20th]* century, had a dog of that name (not a Schipperke) and it called up very happy memories for her of when she had sailed with Uncle Tom, as he was called, during the summer months. They had visited North America and the Mediterranean, including Turkey and Russia. Actually it was in Russia that my grandparents first met.

My grandmother had been a very determined lady. At the age of 17 she had gone to the Crimea from Redruth, where she had been born, to take up a job as children's governess. She had many memories of life in Russia before the turn of the century, one of the most poignant being that of seeing gangs of poor devils being dragged through the streets on their way to Siberia. It must have been a terrible experience for such a young English girl. She out-lived my grandfather by 25 years and died at the age of 93, game to the end and still regularly following the Stock Exchange reports in the *Daily Telegraph*.

From Middlewich we would take the same route by which we had come – 52 miles and 33 locks. It was now Saturday afternoon and if all went well, we could be at Stourport by Tuesday or Wednesday. We were climbing the Audlem flight on Sunday afternoon when we found ourselves greeted by Mr C. M. Marsh. It was nice to see him again - not this time in his official capacity as Divisional Waterways Officer, but out with his family for a Sunday picnic. We had, of course, last seen him at Fradley on the salt run. It had been a wonderful late spring day. We tied up that evening a little above and clear of Tyrley Top Lock.

Columba was running well and *Uranus* was proving easy to handle, all evidence that we had loaded the boats well. The brass was clean, the boats had been washed down and looked beautiful in the early evening light. After supper, just as we were thinking of turning in, we felt a movement of the boats and out of the night came a Cowburn and Cowpar horse-boat. We bade them "good night" and they tied up at the head of the lock ready for the morning.

We were woken the next morning at 5.30

by the rattle of a paddle dropping. The Cowburn and Cowpar were on the move. After a mug of tea and breakfast, we too were on our way again by seven o'clock or so, hoping to arrive at Wheaton Aston Lock in the early afternoon. As the pound was along one of 18 miles, it would have been rather tiring for one person to be at the tiller for six hours at a stretch. We arranged to have a change-over and the easiest way to do this was at two bridge holes, using the bike.

We got to Wheaton Aston in time to catch the shop and stocked up well with eggs, milk, bread, cheese and other necessities. We tied up that night on the Staffordshire and Worcestershire at Compton Wharf, having covered 27 miles. It was then about 6 o'clock, and after our main meal of the day we turned in.

Readers will remember that when we had first gone down the Staffordshire and Worcestershire the previous summer, we had had the assistance of two chaps and a horse. This time we were on our own. I was never able to discover from where the assistance had come. It had arrived absolutely on cue as we were going through Compton Lock. On that earlier occasion, although we had come from Ellesmere Port without any trouble, we were no longer in the area of the North-West Division, but the South-West. I could later think of four possible reasons why the help was supplied. The first was that we were new to the canal. The second was that *Columba*, although a small Woolwich, was bigger than the craft which usually used this canal, and did have twenty tons on board. The third was that *Columba* was owned and skippered by a new-fangled sort of Number One who would probably get stuck anyway. The fourth reason that I could think of was that it was a dry summer and the water was low, which might have caused problems. Most likely it was a combination of all of these reasons, but to the question, "Who organised it, and from where,and how did they know about us?" I still have no answers.

This time we were not having any problems as *Columba* was not getting stuck and *Uranus* was following along very nicely on her short snubber. We were managing the single locks very well, considering the relative inexperience of the crew. The Staffordshire and Worcestershire was a complete change from the Shroppie. Locks presented themselves in a comparatively haphazard manner, with few flights or great vistas. Where locks did occur in flights, there were seldom more than two or three of them. The cut was, in fact, a typical contour canal. The only consistency seemed to be that the locks were all roughly of the same drop, and of course were downhill from Aldersley. With 31 locks in the 25 miles from Compton to Stourport, it would probably take us the better part of two days.

We encountered a single horse-boat coming from Kidderminster, so that he had all the locks ready for us, which made things a bit easier. But it behove us to carry on with the best speed we could muster, because we did not know who was coming behind us. There must have been other boats which had been loaded from that Manchester liner. In any case, we did not want to hang around if we could possibly avoid it, but to get unloaded as quickly as possible at Stourport. From here it was my intention to go down river to Worcester and then up to Burton-on-Trent by train to look at, and perhaps to purchase, two ex-Flixborough Shipping Company boats that I had been told about.

Chapter Eight

EXPANDING

The firm which was offering the boats for sale (the Flixborough Shipping Company) had been one of the subsidiaries of the Grand Union Canal Carrying Company. It was formed before the war to handle trade on the bottom end of the Trent and Mersey Canal and, occasionally, down to the Grand Union. At this time the fleet consisted of three pairs; of these, three motors were up for sale and their three buttys were being taken into the main British Waterways fleet. The motors, big Woolwich built boats, were *Dunstable*, *Epsom* and *Bath*. I do not recollect what the three buttys were, but I suspect that they were big Ricky wooden buttys.

With nationalisation, the policy had been to get rid of the two or three subsidiary companies which was why these boats were for sale. I was asked if I wanted to buy them at £350 each which, on the face of it, seemed to be a ridiculously low figure, particularly as I had seen them working on the few occasions when they had appeared on the Grand Union during the previous year and assessed them to be in fair condition. About a month or so previously, I had been to see an uncle of mine in Worcester and he had agreed to put up a maximum of £700 as a loan. Now all that was required was for me to go to Horninglow, the Headquarters of the Flixborough Shipping Company, to make the inspection and the final decision as to whether to purchase or not.

The first night on the Staffordshire and Worcestershire, we tied up at Kinver and the second at Stourport. On Wednesday morning, we were under way early and tied up at the D & IWE Depot at New Ground ready for unloading. This did not go as smoothly as we had hoped. As on previous occasions, we had to wait, in spite of being the first arrival, for lorries and other road vehicles to be handled first. As a result of this, we did not finish discharging until Thursday morning. We had breasted up before leaving Stourport and had remained so whilst discharging. This was possible because the crane doing the job had been designed to span two boats.

Immediately we were empty, we set off for Worcester, arriving there just after midday. I was now faced with the difficult decision as to which of the boys to take with me to Burton-on-Trent. Both wanted to go, but obviously one would have to stay and look after *Columba* and *Uranus*, so one would be disappointed. It seemed to me that Tom, who had been with me longer, would be better able to cope with any situation that might arise at Worcester, and that Bob, from his experience at nautical training school and the fact that he was better at handling boats than Tom, would be more use to me inspecting *Epsom* and *Dunstable*; so I decided to take Bob and leave Tom at Worcester. It was not easy and I felt that by leaving Tom I was displaying my trust in him, but I know it rankled with him.

The next day, having made sure that the two boats were securely moored at Diglis Basin, Bob and I set off for Worcester Shrub Hill Station to catch the train to Birmingham New Street and thence on to Burton-on-Trent.

When we arrived on Friday afternoon we had a shock. The three boats were in a complete shambles - cabins open, side cloths hanging over the sides and needing renewing, no top cloths, rust and decay everywhere. Never have I seen anything so scruffy. However, they were boats, and even in this condition they were worth having at £350 each.

I had arranged that after our inspection on Friday, if we decided to have them, we would take them on Saturday morning and the money could be paid over after we had moved them. My credit with D & IWE was good and, in any case, we were hardly likely to take the boats out of the country!

Epsom appeared to be the best of the three, and after an inspection we managed to get her engine going. However, we could make no impression on *Dunstable*'s engine, and *Bath* was quite hopeless. We contented ourselves with a bit of squaring up and set off back to Horninglow. We then booked into a pub near the boats and after a supper of tea, bacon and eggs, we turned in. There were five single beds in a bare room just like a school dormitory (remember, this was 1950). Bob's comment was, "Bloody hell, it's like being back at nautical school!" I was most certainly reminded of my prep school in Eastbourne St. Anthony's.

You may be wondering why we were spending good money on a room when we had two cabins at our disposal on the boats. Even if we had had bedclothes, we would not have dared to use those cabins, as they were crawling with bed bugs and lice and would need to be thoroughly disinfected before they would be habitable.

Next morning, we were up early and after breakfast returned to the boats. We scrounged some rope and made two short straps so that *Epsom* could tow *Dunstable*. Luckily the weather was warm and dry so we stopped off at a farm and bought a bundle of hay from which we made a kind of nest in *Epsom's* fore-end in which we could sleep the night.

On left - *Epsom* (later renamed *Kenelm* by John Knill) in Flixborough Shipping Company livery.

Epsom's engine performed really well and we arrived in the Potteries around midday on Monday having done 31 miles with 26 locks since Horninglow. I had, some weeks before, contacted Mr. Shirley of the Mersey, Weaver and Ship Canal Carrying Company to inform him I was thinking of buying, and would want the boats refitted. It was now only a question of ringing him up and soon he was greeting us at the company's docks at Etruria. I think he was rather shaken when he saw the condition of the two boats. We just handed them over and made our way to Stoke Station to catch the train back to Worcester. Later, I was to return to the yard to discuss the refit in more detail.

Tom welcomed us with a good meal when we got back and we set off early the next morning up the Worcester and Birmingham. This was to be done empty, which was a pity, but it was really not worth waiting around on the off chance that a load would turn up; which event might be a matter of some days or even weeks away. I stopped off in Birmingham to visit Parker, Winder and Achurch, the ironmongers, to buy a cabin stove for either *Epsom* or *Dunstable* as we were one short. I did not get a range, mainly because they did not have a suitable one. The stove I purchased was finished in mottled green enamel, of the usual florid Victorian design, with two sliding doors and a small, openable hot-plate. We could get by with this quite adequately.

We then made our way back to Anderton as quickly as possible for more loading orders. Here we were told that there would be two or three days wait, so the next morning I took the opportunity to go down to Mersey Weaver again to settle details of the overhaul. When I got back to the dock I found that, as I had surmised, *Epsom*'s condition was not too bad, but that *Dunstable* was in a bad state.

I asked Mr. Shirley to press on with *Epsom*, which I had decided to rename *Kenelm*. This was partly due to a misunderstanding on my part, as I thought *Columba* had been named after a British saint (so much for my knowledge of Astronomy). As my second name is Kenelm, also that of a British saint, I thought this would be most appropriate. I was influenced in this by the fact that my family was Roman Catholic and had always gravitated towards British saints instead of the more popular French or Italian variety. I had been christened Kenelm after my godfather, Kenelm Powell, brother of Sebastian Pugin Powell, the uncle who had loaned me the money for the purchase of the boats. Their elder brother was Dunstan Powell, so what more natural then to rename *Dunstable* as *Dunstan* at the same time'? (These three Powells were grandsons of Augustus Welby Pugin, the great Victorian architect).

I had heard by now a rumour that another salt run was in the wind for mid-summer. Also, from my seat on the IWA Council, I knew about the rally of narrow boats that was planned at the Market Harborough Festival. It would be pleasant if these two events could be combined.

For the time being, we continued with *Columba* and *Uranus* carrying cargoes between points in the North-Western Division and Birmingham which was quite hard work with a butty, as we had to negotiate so many single locks in the Birmingham area. Still, many other boatmen were doing this and so could we.

We discovered that there had been problems on the Kennet and Avon Canal. It seemed that the D & IWE South-Western Division was becoming alarmed at the number of craft using the canal. This paradoxical situation arose from the fact that commercial craft had the statutory right to navigation on the canal and, with the terrible state of the way, it had cost British Railways quite a bit in rescue operations. Pleasure craft, not having these rights of navigation, could be left to their own devices if they got stuck, but not so the working boats. The Great Western Railway had been caught on the hop in 1948, just before nationalisation, when Gerry Bird and Bill Bennett in *Westminster*,with ten tons of grain from Avonmouth on board, had worked their way through the Kennet and Avon to Hovis at Newbury. It had been very expensive for the Great Western because they had had to throw in a lot of their resources to get *Westminster* through the result of years of neglect. The fact that the boat's owner was William Gilchrist

Bennett, a solicitor who was well aware of the obligations of the Great Western, meant that they were unable to side-step their responsibilities.

It was unfortunate that this had not happened some time before, but I suppose the advent of World War II had prevented any sort of similar activity. But what a boon the canal would have been during the war if it had been in good condition and properly navigable. Commercial traffic had ceased in 1935 when Robbins, Lane and Pinniger of Honey Street (on the canal bank) ceased their timber shipments from Avonmouth.

British Railways was able to pass that particular buck over to the Docks and Inland Waterways Executive when it was formed. They were given a taste of what was in store for them when John Gould decided to use the canal for carrying, possibly fired by my success after buying *Columba* and *Uranus*.

John purchased from A. Harvey-Taylor, of Aylesbury, a pair of old wooden boats, still in good condition, *Colin* and *Iris*. He had moved them quickly down to Newbury and the South-Western Division woke up to discover that they had a viper in their bosom, so to speak. The situation was made infinitely worse (in their eyes) by the fact that John Gould was not just doing various local jobs, but was also bringing coal from the Midlands Coalfield with the full support of the South-Eastern Division.

One can imagine the chagrin of the boys at Gloucester when this was followed by the formation of the Newbury Branch of the Inland Waterways Association, of which I was a founder member. The Chairman of the Newbury Branch was none other than John Lester, for whom I had delivered the cargo of salt for Newbury Laundry.

The South-Western Division, already alarmed at John Gould's activities and my first salt run (we were costing them money!), were further disturbed when rumours of more extensive activities on the Kennet and Avon began to circulate. Firstly, the distinct possibility of more, and larger salt runs. In spite of the prophecies of the Jeremiahs, the cargo had arrived in good condition at Newbury, with great satisfaction to the customer. The Cerebos salesman had actually persuaded others besides John Lester to have their salt delivered by canal. It was planned to increase the assignment to 40 tons using two motor boats, and to include in the cargo not only rough salt for the laundry work but also table and cooking salt for grocers in the area. This was a great admission of faith and confidence in me, as the block and table salt had to be delivered in prime condition and they were obviously convinced that I could do it. The second factor was John Gould's desire to increase his activities as well.

All this was too much for the South-Western Division. Instead of welcoming the resurgence of life on the canal (it was, after all, what the D & IWE were supposed to be promoting), they awoke from their rather cosy sleep and decided to close the canal! Their spurious grounds for this was that urgent maintenance was required. This was a polite fiction and an attempt (successful as it turned out) to close the actual canal without going to the considerable effort of obtaining an Act of Parliament, which was the legal requirement. They relied on the fact that any action anyone took to combat their lethargy would take so long that, by the time it was achieved, it would be too late. This is exactly, what happened. John Gould brought a court case for loss of traffic because of the D & IWE's panic-stricken and arbitrary actions but, by the time the action had dragged its painfully slow way through court, the canal had been closed for so long that it was no

Tom Foxon steering *Kenelm*, newly docked and with experimental blue livery.

longer possible to reopen it. It remained so for 26 years and was only reopened through the concentrated effort of private individuals working through the Kennet and Avon Canal Trust and not through the Government body whose job it really was.

The sad part of this was that the D & IWE seems to have been a rather uncoordinated organisation, in that the North-Western and South-Eastern Divisions were granting me special tolls for carrying over canals in their Divisions (Trent & Mersey in the North-West, and the Coventry Canal, the Birmingham & Fazeley Canal and the Oxford Canal in the South-East) at the same time as the South-West was trying to do away with carrying traffic.

Meanwhile, with all this drama taking place down south, we were up north trying to run a pair of boats and a business, blissfully unaware of what was going on.

At this time, I had been proposed for membership of the National Association of Inland Waterways Carriers. I had known about this group before I joined, mainly through the IWA Council. We had the impression that the NAIWC was mainly interested in the carriers in the large waterways up north,including the Manchester Ship Canal and their shipping line. In fact, the Secretary was an employee of the Bridgewater Canal Company (a subsidiary of the Ship Canal) and he treated narrow boat owners with what I think may be called scorn. What any of the owners got out of NAIWC, except a receipt for their subscription and an occasional newsletter, I never really discovered.

I had joined mainly in the hope that there would be some dissemination of news (on cargoes, for instance) between members but there did not seem to anything of this nature involved. It was certainly absent from the newsletter which would have been the sensible place for information of this kind to circulated. Meanwhile, life was beginning to get hectic. My first concern was to make sure that the boats were available whenever cargoes materialised. This was proving to be not so often as I had hoped, but we were not doing too badly. I had two disappointments, both concerning back-loading. There was little or none from Birmingham for the north, nor any to Worcester and Stourport, which meant that we were frequently running empty.

I was also beginning to realise that our strongest opposition was not coming from the railways, but from road transport. This was especially so once 'C' licences had been virtually done away with. Like the railways, boats were long distance carriers, and we were both being hurt. I have mentioned before the way in which boat loading or discharging was always delayed or interrupted when a lorry appeared.

This practice mitigated against the efficiency of canal carriers and it caused great dissatisfaction amongst boats' crews. Many felt, as I did myself, that this attitude was perpetrated through the weakness or disinterest of the D & IWE employees, who should have been more concerned with loyalty to their fellow employees of D & IWE, whether direct or subcontract.

Two other concerns were exercising me at this time. The first was to get down to Etruria as often as possible in order to put pressure on Mersey Weavers to get *Kenelm* finished as soon as possible. The second concern was what to do about *Dunstable* or, as she would be known from now on, *Dunstan*. As so often happens, this difficulty was overcome in a most unexpected way. I had brought *Columba* and *Uranus* to Middlewich with 45 tons of tomato puree, had tied up and then went on my way to the yard by bus. During the bus journey the solution to the problem suddenly flashed across my mind and I jotted it down there and then on the only piece of paper I had available - the back of my bus ticket.

The difficulty was that *Dunstan*'s timber gunwales had been badly twisted, so her sides were considerably out of shape. She had obviously been badly cross-winded going into single locks, either through negligence or through having to manoeuvre in high winds; in view of her general condition, the former seemed the more likely. The gunwales, not only split but rotten in many places, would have to be replaced throughout. They were oak beams, scarfed every eight or ten feet, and bolted to the angle at the top of the sides. Replacing them in the usual way with three or four ten-foot lengths would have done nothing to straighten the sides permanently.

The "bus ticket solution" I have reproduced here, as nearly as I can (I no longer have the original ticket, needless to say!)

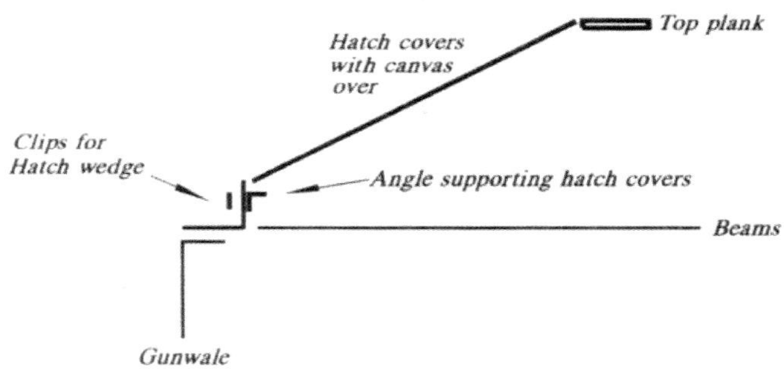

My answer was to use six-inch steel angle bolted to the angle at the top of the sides and to use the angle as the basis for fitting hatch covers. The steel would undoubtedly be more expensive than timber, but not unduly so, for the oak had to be shaped and scarfed, which would take time and therefore money. Also, the overall weight of *Dunstan* would go up a bit but her sides would be straight and I might even be producing a prototype for the narrow boat of the future.

To say that Mr. Shirley was aghast at such a revolutionary concept was to put it mildly, but he was so dumbfounded that he did not attempt to argue. It was agreed that my proposals would be put into operation.

The yard had got on very well with *Kenelm*. The engine had had a top overhaul and was working fine. In another week she would be ready to be collected. She had already been painted and lettered and the only thing needed was varnishing. The colour scheme was slightly different from *Columba* and *Uranus* in that, whilst the stiles had been grained in light oak with a green frame inside, the main panels were in dark royal blue upon which was yellow lettering with green shading. The lettering was the same format as the other boats but instead of their Roman, Shirley had chosen Egyptian(similar to that used by GWR). In her new colours, her cabin all scrubbed out, grained in light oak and varnished, what a difference she presented from the grubby boat we had picked up at Horninglow.

As luck would have it, our next journey would take more than a week, so that the earliest we could come and pick up *Kenelm* would be the second weekend after my visit. This would mean our having to get to Sampson Road and back in ten days, including discharging. It looked as though we would be travelling through the night again.

When we got to Autherley, there was a letter waiting for me from the North-Western Division alerting me to the fact that there was another salt run in the offing. It confirmed that the cargo would be picked up from Cerebos, at Middlewich, and would be about 40 tons. Because of the decision of the South-Western Division to "carry out repairs", the unloading would have to take place in Reading. I promptly wrote off to John Gould asking him to contact the Cerebos agent. By the time I had gone to Brum, discharged the tomato puree and returned to Autherley, there was another letter waiting, this time confirming that the load would include block and powder salt for the grocers in Reading and Newbury District, as well as the rough salt we had handled before.

Ever since the first salt run, I had felt that the way we had discharged then could be improved. There must be a better way than unloading by hand onto a truck, wheeling up a plank and man-handling it onto a lorry. This method seemed a bit antiquated for the middle Fifties of the Twentieth Century. It had sufficed for a trial run, but now that it looked as it salt runs were to become a regular feature, it seemed sensible to employ a less cumbersome method.

What was needed was some kind of hoist to lift the sacks straight out of the boats and deposit them on the lorry. After a little looking around at what was available, I decided to purchase a petrol-driven hoist made by Tasker's of Andover. It was small, something like a ship's anchor davit, with the petrol engine mounted onto it and connected to a hydraulic pump. This, with a piston and cylinder via a system of pulleys, could handle loads of around one and a half hundredweights. The hoist was completely portable. The foot of the davit (which had an overall weight of about one and a half hundredweights), was designed to fit into a specially adapted socket which could be mounted into the floor at the rear of the lorry or trailer. Once fitted, this socket allowed the hoist to move through 360 degrees.

The operation was simple. The lorry backed up to overhang the boat and the engine of the hoist was started. A sack could be hauled up using a rope strap placed round its neck and packages could be hung to the hook of the hoist. The control consisted of a single lever.

We now had to find a compliant carrier, preferably a coal merchant, who had several lorries so that one would always be available to us when we needed it. Our stipulations were that the firm should be one whose lorries were kept clean and tidy, that they would be willing to have the sockets fitted and that they would agree to carry on the roof of the cab a bold sign, in bright red on chrome yellow, reading "Use Inland Waterways", the slogan I also had painted in white letters on the boats' black top cloths. We selected a co-operative coal merchant to whom Tasker's were asked to deliver the hoist and sockets.

The time-table was now beginning to hot up. On arrival at Middlewich once more, I left Tom in charge of *Columba* and *Uranus* whilst Bob and I set off by bus to Etruria to collect *Kenelm*. Here we set about buying essentials for equipping her - mattress, army blankets, pillows, crockery, cutlery, bucket, saucepan, frying pan and, of course, food. Water can, ropes and fuel had been supplied by the dock. In a moment of inspiration, a torch was added to our supplies. *Kenelm* was already fitted with electric light for the cabin, run from batteries. By the time everything was stowed away it was a Saturday morning, and we were all ready to go when we were told that the Harecastle Tunnel did not operate at weekends. What was more, as Monday was a Bank Holiday, it would actually be Tuesday before the next tug journey took place. We explained our predicament and time-table to the Tunnel Inspector and he said we could go through on our own. I must confess that there were times on that trip when I wished that he had said "No"!

I should explain that a big Woolwich motor is a very large boat. When empty it lies by the stern with the bow high in the air. Because of the weight of the engine and about 140 gallons of fuel, the stern would be drawing about two feet nine to three feet six inches, whilst the bow would only be drawing about six inches. The maximum headroom in the tunnel was given in the 1904 Handbook as eight feet ten inches, but in the *Bradshaw* for 1928, this had been reduced to six feet four inches. Here we were, another 26 years later, when almost certainly further subsidence had taken place. On reflection, I decided that this was probably the true reason why we had been allowed through on our own. The Inspector had probably thought that there would have been problems if we snagged the roof when we were one of a line of boats pulled by the electric tug.

We entered the south end of the tunnel, and for the first 400 yards we managed pretty well. After this was where my purchase of the electric torch proved to be an inspiration, as we could shine this fairly powerful lamp ahead of us on the roof of the tunnel to help us judge our alignment. The light was augmented by opening the doors of the engine hole, where we had a hurricane lamp, and by the light coming from the newly installed electric lamp in the cabin.

The towpath was cantilevered from the side of the tunnel (it was rather similar to the towpath on Telford's masterpiece, the Pontcysyllte Aqueduct) and one of the obvious signs of subsidence to be seen was where this structure had collapsed in places. Bob was much lighter than me, so it seemed sensible to hand over the steering to him whilst I went up with the torch to the fore-end of the hold where some extra weight would help. Before we entered the tunnel, we had taken the precaution of removing everything that was possible. The cratch was dismantled, the mast box was lying in the bottom of the boat; the stands, exhaust pipe and chimney had also been removed, and we were considering whether it would be necessary to remove the pigeon box.

So close were we to the roof that Bob was

having to steer in a crouched position. I was doing my best to handle the torch in such a way as to avoid the boat hitting the roof. To minimise any possible damage, we had reduced speed from four to less than two miles an hour. We were constantly aware that if we hit the roof hard it might cause a major collapse. That one and five eighths miles took more than two hours; and an anxious two hours they were.

We had entered the southern end in daylight; the light somewhat dimmed by an overcast sky. When we eventually emerged, it was quite dark and beginning to drizzle. There seemed to be no point in pushing on in these conditions so we decided to tie up for the night at Red Bull Wharf, near the summit of the six Red Bull Locks. We cooked a quick meal and were glad to get to bed. Although we had travelled only about six miles with six locks, it had been a tiring day, made even more so by the anxiety imposed by negotiating the tunnel.

The next morning we left early. The weather improved and by early afternoon. we had arrived back at *Columba* and *Uranus* after a journey of 10 miles and 24 locks. Not only was Tom glad to see us back, so was Bosun. By this point, both Tom and Bob had become very fond of him and Tom had found him good company whilst we were away.

There was no immediate prospect of loading for the Shroppie nor any sign of the salt. We informed the Liverpool Office of the D & IWE that we were staying put for a while, and began squaring up *Kenelm*. As a reminder of our Harecastle adventure, we discovered quite a quantity of rubble and soot in *Kenelm's* bottom. We reassembled the cratch, which had not yet been done. The sidestrings and top strings were properly spliced into their respective eyelets. All in all, we were quite busy. With the bright colours on the new boat, all the brass brightly polished and the rope work and strings properly scrubbed white on all three boats, the whole display was most certainly eye-catching.

We had decided to pair *Columba* with *Kenelm* rather than with *Uranus* for this trip, to give Bob additional experience in charge of a motor. We would find the advantage of this on the salt run when it materialised, as he would have to cope with both single locks and the River Thames. (Using *Uranus* we should have breasted up, but with *Kenelm* we should use the motors of both boats.) We transferred the black top cloths and tippets from *Uranus* to *Kenelm*, and put the new green ones from the refit on to *Uranus*.

Whilst all this was going on, we had news that the salt run was now definite; it would be some time the following week. It was now Wednesday and the middle of June, and it was left for me to make arrangements with Cerebos. The Market Harborough Rally had been fixed for a week beginning on the 14th August, and I was still hoping to attend as a member of the IWA with one or more of my boats. With reasonable weather conditions, we should have none of the flood problems on the Oxford Canal and the River Thames that we had experienced last time, so we should have every chance of getting to the Rally. We should not waste money having to hang around and might even get some back-loading from the Kennet & Avon if we were lucky.

By 9.30 am on the Thursday morning, we were waiting at the Cerebos factory for loading to begin. Things began to move at about eleven o'clock, when we decided to start by putting 20 tons of salt on *Columba* first. Once this was aboard, the blocks of cooking salt and bags of granulated or crystal salt were loaded into *Kenelm*. The blocks were seven or eight inches square and about 18 inches long. They were

Uranus

wrapped in stiff paper and had to be handled carefully to avoid cracking them. For the same reason they also had to be stacked in such a way that they would not be subjected to any violent jolts or shocks. The cooking salt was in bags of fine linen, each containing about 56 pounds. The surplus bag salt went into *Kenelm*, but we had to take great care to make sure it did not come into contact with the more refined salts. Another complication was that this time the cargo was to be distributed to several different firms, so we had to try to keep the various consignments separate. Luckily, *Kenelm* had a bigger hold than *Columba* and it was possible to stack leaving spaces between. Unfortunately, the sacks were not labelled with the names of the recipients - these were only given on our chits. This meant we had to be very careful about our paperwork.

As each boat was loaded, the side cloths were unrolled from the gunwales, the side strings tied and the top cloths fitted. It was lucky that the weather was dry, as this made loading so much easier. Had it been raining, or even threatening to, the boats would have had to be sheeted up first. Then a considerable amount of juggling would have had to take place as we loaded through the top cloths to make sure that the cargo itself and the floor-boards were kept as dry as possible.

Our last salt run had been in a very wet winter period and even so, we had got stuck, so it was behoven to us to have the boats as light as possible, especially for the first part as far as Hawkesbury. Although *Columba* would take a total of 120 gallons of fuel and *Kenelm* 140, we decided not to fill them up. Hawkesbury was about 80 miles away - a distance that would use up roughly 80 gallons - so the tank in each boat was kept down to 90 gallons in order to save weight. We reasoned that drawing this much we would be much less likely to get stuck in the bottom end of the Trent and Mersey through Rugeley and Armitage.

Once loaded, we moved off to a more acceptable spot to spend the night, towing *Uranus*. We spent a little while transferring everything moveable, including food and cooking gear, into *Columba* and *Kenelm* so that we could tow *Uranus* to the Mersey Weaver yard at Etruria and leave her there completely empty. On our return from Reading, we planned to pick her up with the newly re-fitted *Dunstan*. A new problem would then arise - one of manning three boats and one butty with a crew of only three. However, this would not arise for another three or four months and perhaps by then the difficulty would have resolved itself.

Having *Uranus* with us for the first part of the journey had both its advantages and disadvantages. We would be going through Harecastle again, which might be difficult. We had decided that the two motors should go first in line. The first would be no problem to steer, but the second, with *Uranus* behind her, would have her steerability limited to some degree. *Uranus*, although only a small Woolwich, was a big boat for this kind of manoeuvring. As events, turned out, we got through with no snags.

It was quite tough working the three boats down to Etruria with only the three of us and slow, too. Middlewich to Etruria is only 18 miles, but there are thirty-odd locks to deal with. We were helped somewhat by the fact that 24 of them were duplicate locks.

This system was an expedient devised by James Brindley to save water. Each lock was, in fact, two locks side by side. I have mentioned this arrangement before, but perhaps a fuller account of their working would not be out of place here. We were coming downhill, and the left-hand locks were full. The boats goes in, then instead of opening the paddles on the bottom gates, as would happen in a normal lock,the centre paddle is lifted to let the water into the right-hand lock.

When the locks are equalised, the centre paddle is lowered. Next, the bottom paddle of the left-hand lock is raised and, at the same time, so is the top paddle of the right-hand lock. In this way, the left-hand is emptying and the right-hand is filling at the same time. When empty, the bottom gate of the left-hand lock opens to allow the boat through, whilst the top gate of the right-hand lock admits the second boat to that lock. Using this method about half a lock of water (some 20,000 gallons) is saved on each lock operation. I believe Brindley was the only canal builder who employed duplicate narrow locks, the others being three at Hillmorton on the Oxford Canal. (There are duplicate locks on the London Regents Canal, but these are large locks to accommodate barges but on the same principle.)

Compared with the first salt run back in February, this was proving to be a much more pleasant experience. The weather was better and the going much smoother. Even Rugeley and Armitage, where we had so much trouble last time, were passed without difficulty. There was, too, no fear of floods in the area of Brindley Banks.

It was not until we were on the Birmingham and Fazeley Canal that we had any real problem. This was at Tamworth (Glascote), outside S. E. Barlow's yard. Problem is perhaps too strong a word to use, as we were simply slowed down, but not enough to hold us up for very long. Soon we were up Atherstone and at Hawkesbury.

We fuelled up at the *Greyhound* and stocked up at the shop. We had a brief word with Miss Edwards at the Boat Control and were gauged by Mr Pitt. After all this we were on our way and we tied up that night at the place which was known as "Noble" - even if it was spelt "Newbold". We wanted to be in the Tunnel the next night or at any rate, clear of Napton Top Lock. It would be better if we could get to the top of Claydon. With luck, we should without extending ourselves greatly, be able to get to Cropredy in plenty of time to get a supply of their bacon and get our first view this trip of the Cherwell, which played such a dramatic part in our journey of six months before. Now that we were not quite as pushed by the conditions, I could also remember that here at Cropredy, astride the infant Cherwell, was fought one of the opening battles of the Civil War in 1644.

This time through Banbury we did not see Tom Rolt's *Cressy*, because by the time we passed she was tied up at Gayton on her way to what was to prove for him the ill-fated Market Harborough Rally. This was to prove a wounding event to the Inland Waterways

Association, but I will deal with this more thoroughly later on.

What a difference there was this time! Beautiful weather and no floods made it seem like another canal altogether. Once again we visited the signal box to get the bridge swung, and this time there was no fuss or waiting. Soon we were in Osney Lock and so down the Thames to Abingdon. The lock-keeper here remembered us and I saw that the nick in the stonework made by *Columba's* bows was still very noticeable.

It was really beautiful on the Thames, and this had attracted a large number of pleasure boats out on to the river. We were greeted with stares; they obviously thought of us as a very unusual pair of craft going down the river in line ahead. Our horn was in pretty constant use because of the number of people who either did not know the rule of the road or, knowing it, did not think it mattered. Thank goodness there was a number of people who did know what it was all about.

We were now approaching Mapledurham on one of the more beautiful stretches of the Thames. The river here is gloriously wide with islands and channels in its midst. We moved on to Reading and once more gained the entrance to the Kennet & Avon Canal through County Lock. We tied up at Bear Wharf at midday and telephoned the Cerebos agent. Unloading would begin next morning soon after nine o'clock. The lorry with their fittings for the hoist was alerted, and we bought petrol for its engine. Fortunately the weather forecast was good, but we decided that in spite of that we would not unsheet until the following day, just in case of a mishap like a rainstorm creeping up from nowhere.

At nine o'clock, the lorries arrived and unloading went well. The first boat was empty soon after midday and we were completely through by mid-morning of the following day. We now had the possibility of a cargo to take to Hampton, 50 miles down the Thames. This was to be special top soil for T. Harrison Chaplin, the riparian firm. This cargo, when it arrived, was loaded at Bear Wharf by tipping. It was then levelled out and sheeted up. We used the slack boards with *Columba*. The all-up weight was about 45 tons on the pair.

We started moving the next day and spent the night at Marlow Lock. The weather was fine and the river was running fast. *Columba* led, as we had a klaxon. Going over the salt run and discharging, everything had gone very well. The lorries and the drivers had been there to time, the drivers had been very helpful and the hoist had exceeded all expectations. We restricted it to around one hundred weight and by doing so, were able to speed up the discharge. So enthusiastic were we all that it almost seemed like the dawn of a new age, at any rate for the small carrier, who, we thought, could now take jobs which before would have been tedious or hard work because of the unloading. The Tasker hoist could also be used for loading. We were to put it to a further test with the discharging of our top-soil.

We were away from Marlow the next morning and ran down to Hampton where we arrived late that afternoon. It was an interesting if uneventful run, taking us through some glorious scenery and outstanding places. I had been over Brunel's beautiful bridge at Maidenhead on many occasions, each time passing it in a matter of seconds. It was lovely to be able to go under it almost at leisure and to appreciate the genius that had prompted it. Other highlights were the numerous locks, all marvellously kept and each of which we "had help" going through, and the impressive grandeur of Windsor Castle on the bend of the river.

We arrived at Hampton Parish Wharf in the late afternoon and got ready for discharging the next morning. We had brought the hoist and socket with us, not with any definite plan to use them, but just in case they might be handy. To begin with, the unloading went very badly. Chaplins had given us one or two men to help, but it was slow, back-breaking work shovelling the cargo to the height of the Wharf. Then I had a brain wave. The lorry we were using had a very bad plank floor, but it might work. I got permission from Chaplin's to cut a hole near the tail gate where the hoist could be fitted. We borrowed a couple of dustbins and with the aid of some rope straps, we soon had the hoist operating. It worked like a dream. Each time we were lifting a three-quarter full dustbin, which was a jolly sight better than shovelling. It was not too many hours before we had *Kenelm* empty.

Unloading topsoil from *Columba* at Shepperton on River Thames using Taskers of Andover hoist.
Photos: Jack Gashion

Before we had left Bear Wharf, I had decided that Hampton would probably be a good place to get an official photograph of the newly-docked *Kenelm*. I had contacted Jack Gashion once again (the man who had photographed *Columba* in 1949). So whilst we were finishing off discharging *Columba*, Tom washed down *Kenelm* and got her ready for the photographs. I had asked Jack Gashion to meet us at Hampton and during the day after we arrived he duly turned up.

The whole set-up looked very smart. Tom had donned a crisp, white tee-shirt and black beret. Two photographs were taken, one a very good three-quarter stern view with Tom well in evidence as he brought *Kenelm* astern. The other was a full-length beam-on shot. Jack had to go to the other

Kenelm at Shepperton, with Tom Foxon

side of the river in order to be able to show *Kenelm*'s full length, but it was worth it as it produced a fine photograph which served to show what a workmanlike craft a large Woolwich motor was. For these photographs, I had borrowed *Columba*'s funnel, but in due course I was to have another funnel made for *Kenelm*. What with the morning hiccough over the unloading and the photography, we did not get finished that day so our departure was held over for another day.

On completion, we set off down river for Brentford. There was always the possibility that we might get some back-loading. A cargo for Birmingham or better still, Northampton would have been fine, but the ideal would have been something for Leicester, as we were on our way to Market Harborough. Unfortunately, loading for Leicester was becoming exceedingly rare. There had in the past been canal trade to Market Harborough itself but this was now non-existent. I had hopes that one of the results of our visit to the rally might help to drum up some interest here. It might be possible, for instance, to bring raw materials from London Docks for Symington Soups, somewhat on the lines of the Fellows, Morton and Clayton traffic to H. P. Sauce in Birmingham.

All this time I had been a member of the IWA and had a seat on the Council. I attended meetings whenever I could at 11 Gower Street, but it was an understood thing that I would only attend whenever I was in that end of the canal system. This had been easier to arrange when I was using the Grand Union Canal in my early days, but now I was using the Shroppie and other canals it was sometimes more difficult for me to attend meetings.

When I first joined the IWA the constitution laid down the aims as "advocating the maintenance, development and use of our rivers and canals both for waterborne trade and as national amenities". Our Small Boaters' Committee was struggling to put flesh on this framework.

Early on in the planning stages of the Market Harborough Rally, various ideas for trophies to be awarded for various achievements had been postulated; one such suggestion was a cup for the greatest distance covered by a working pair. I offered to present what I hoped would become a Challenge Cup for the best-kept pair of working boats. In the general euphoria of those days I imagined a succession of rallies stretching down through the years and was completely oblivious to the tensions and personality strains that were building up. Obviously, as in any group of people, there were bound to be differences, but I am afraid that I was somewhat naïve about what the outcome of these differences could be. Like everybody else, I had my circle which included Pat Lucan, Tom and Angela Rolt, Sonia Smith and Gerry Bird. We were all people who had practical day-to-day experience of the canals and felt that we knew what had to be done to improve things. We were critical of the IWA's two bêtes-noires, the D & IWE and the National Association of Inland Waterways Carriers (NAIWC), but we did not believe them to be devils incarnate, as the rest of the Council seemed to think. We had to work with them, after all. It was becoming obvious that the cracks were beginning to appear in the fabrics of the IWA. Probably that is why the Small Boaters' Committee drew a sort of carapace of work over itself; a carapace which distanced them from the impending crisis. The only effect of this, as it turned out, was to add to the mistrust which the Chairman and other members of the Council felt. It was taken for granted that at our meetings, not only were we discussing Rome, but we must, ipso facto, be discussing Caesar himself. All in all, this was becoming a deeply unhappy period in my canal odyssey.

To return to the Cup. I had inherited a lot of silverware from my grandfather's estate, amongst which was an unmarked, two-handed cup and stand, which was about 12 inches high. I thought I would present this as the *Columba's Cup*. I felt a bit badly about it not costing me anything, so I decided to have engraved on it the picture which I had drawn for my notepaper and which John Gould subsequently used for the cover of the Kennet and Avon magazine, *The Butty*. With the picture was also the wording *Columba's Cup*. The work was arranged during one of my journeys home, and was beautifully carried out by Halfhide's, the jewellers of Wimbledon Hill Road.

Columba's Cup
Photo: Jack Gashion

Chapter Nine

MARKET HARBOROUGH

After discharging at Hampton Parish Wharf, we set out the next morning for Brentford, a run of just under 20 miles or about four hours. Then, at long last, we should be back on the Grand Union after having been away for about six or seven months. It was nice to think that we would be meeting old friends again. Arriving at Brentford in the late afternoon, we made contact at the office. We were told that a cargo would be available in about 24 hours and as there was likely to be a shortage of boats, there could be work for us if we wished to wait and see. I reckoned there were 10 or 12 days before we were due at Market Harborough, and that we would have nothing to lose by waiting. We fuelled at Bulls Bridge and filled in the time; shopping, getting the boats ready for loading, cleaning the engine room and generally titivating. It so happened that the cargo was ready for us the very next day, but this whole day was wasted (from our point of view) in the loading of the D & IWE vans ahead of us. It looked as if our loading would not be possible until mid-morning of the next day. This was how it worked out, and our cargo turned out to be 45 tons of steel for Tyseley. This was very convenient and not too big a load for our two motors. The weather seemed to be set fine, so it would not be necessary for us to use our top sheets.

We got up to Bulls Bridge before closing time and went on a spending spree, buying new tip cat, bows fender, cabin and long shafts for *Kenelm* and a couple of new cotton lines. Now, with our own skills and hard work, we were prepared to make a good showing when we got to Market Harborough. We made a good run to Brum, unloaded at Tyseley, turned round and went down south through Braunston and its tunnel. By this point we had nearly a whole week in which to get to Market Harborough, so we were able to take it fairly easily. Even so, with two empty motors, we made good time to the top of Watford Locks on the Leicester arm, where we tied up for the night.

The next morning, we went through Crick Tunnel (1,528 yards long) and, just beyond the junction for the Welford Branch, Husbands Bosworth Tunnel (1,166 yards long). Both these tunnels are 16 feet wide and will thus allow two narrow boats to pass, or be sufficiently wide for a wide boat like *Progress*. Watford Locks and Foxton Locks, though, are only seven feet wide. The reason for the mixture of gauges, I think, lies in the early days of canals. The length from Leicester was to be called the Union under the Act of the 33rd of George III (1792-3) and was to run to Northampton, a distance of 43¼ miles, where it joined the River Nene. Like the Soar at Leicester, the Nene was a wide navigation. The canal was subsequently rerouted and incorporated into the Grand Junction. In 1933, when the Grand Junction and the Warwick and Birmingham Canals were amalgamated, the old title of Grand Union was revived. This does not explain the narrow Leicester arm which joins the two wide sections of the canal, any more than it does the narrow Northampton arm, joining the two wide navigations, the Grand Junction main line and the River Nene. It is most likely due to the problems with water supply, which (strange as it may seem given our English climate) has always been a problem on our canals.

An interesting attempt to solve in part the problem of lack of water was the Foxton Inclined Plane, which I mentioned in the previous chapter. This device, after a great deal of ingenuity on the part of the designer and energy on behalf of the builders, lasted in operation for only 11 years. The idea was to take a single boat sideways up a sloping surface, counterbalanced by another boat moving down. What made it uneconomical to run was the fact that it was operated by a steam engine. Whether there was traffic or not, this engine had to be kept fired, so in periods when it was little used, it cost a great deal for practically no return.

In the days of horse boats, I suppose it did not really matter much whether a particular section of canal was narrow or wide. If you were working a single boat, you had one horse, if a pair you had two, so there was really no difference working single or double locks. However, with the advent of steam in the *[eighteen]* eighties and nineties and diesel from about 1912, the disadvantages of single locks became more apparent. By this time, the railways had made such inroads into the canal trade that the expense of widening canals could not be justified.

We arrived at the top of Foxton Locks. The view was absolutely staggering. The countryside seemed to my imagination to look exactly as it might have been 500 years or more before. Foxton has 10 locks in two staircases of five each, and the drop for each lock is only about seven feet. From above it has the appearance of a deeply wooded landscape, with the canal plunging in a sheer drop between the trees.

Columba led the way, and at the bottom of the flight we turned right for the final leg to Market Harborough. The branch is five and three quarter miles long and it seemed very like other canals with very little trade on it. After about three miles, however, there was a great change. There were boats of every conceivable sort, shape and size tied up bow to stern. It seemed that there would be nowhere for us to moor. At last we came to an open berth. Bob and Tom were on *Kenelm* and they decided to tie up there whilst they could, whilst I in *Columba* pushed on to see if there was anywhere else available. If not, I should have to wind and tie up alongside *Kenelm*. We were about half a mile from the end of the canal. I just hoped that the basin would not be jammed full of boats so that winding *Columba*

Kenelm and Columba moored - believed to be at Market Harborough

would be impossible. I really did not fancy retreating stern-first to the junction!

As I approached the basin, I recognised some of the boats moored along the banks. There were Samuel Barlow's *Cairo* and *Warwick*, with George and Sonia Smith on board, a pair of S. E. Barlows, Tom Rolt's *Cressy*, Holt Abbott's new canal-type cabin cruiser, Peter Scott's *Beatrice*, Alf Best's D & IWE pair *Alton and Ayr* and the Ovaltine pair *Mimas* and *Ray* captained by Arthur Stokes. I took a good look at the available space and reckoned that there was enough room in the basin itself to wind *Columba*. There were far too many people looking for my liking - if I did make a hash of it, it would be a very public affair. I made a fairly spectacular entry, then pushed the helm hard over to starboard. Then full astern and helm to port, and we were winding nicely without touching anything. As I passed *Alton*, Alf Best gave some welcome help by jumping on to the fore end with a shaft to push us around to port. Then I was on my way out of the basin, having accomplished the turn very smoothly. I think many of the onlookers on various craft expected me to make a bit of a meal of it and were surprised at how neatly the whole move had been done. It had all been quite exhilarating. I put Alf Best ashore and then returned to where *Kenelm* was moored and tied up alongside with help from the boys. The next item on the agenda was to get a good meal, and whilst eating it, to discuss the next moves. We tied up the boat, polished the brass and did our best to make the pair look as beautiful as possible.

Judging for *Columba's Cup* at Market Harborough. The judges, John Knill and Lord Lucan, are on the right, with the eventual winners, Mr & Mrs Stokes of Ovaltine's *Mimas* and *Ray*.

John Knill announcing the winners of the *Columba's Cup* at the IWA rally at Market Harborough 1950.

After we had finished our work, I walked along the towpath to the basin to call on Tom and Angela Rolt in *Cressy*. Since I had last seen them there had been a sharp deterioration in relations between the Rolts and Robert Aickman, the Chairman of IWA. Aickman had even gone to the extent of telling Tom, whose idea the rally had been, that he would not be welcome at Market Harborough!

This seemed to nearly everybody to be grossly unfair.

When I had said goodbye to Angela and Tom, I moved on to have another chat with George and Sonia Smith on their pair, *Cairo* and *Warwick*. The Smiths, like me, were both surprised and affronted by Robert Aickman's attitude to the Rolts.

I found myself a little disappointed with the response to the competition for the *Columba's Cup*. The entries so far, I discovered, were a pair from Ovaltine, a pair from S. E. Barlow and one from Samuel Barlow. This was a pity, as I had hoped that more firms would have been sufficiently interested to release boats for two or three days. This was not to be. There were no entries from Harvey-Taylor, Fellows Morton, or from Thomas Clayton or Cowburn and Cowpar from the northern canals. The D & IWE had chosen to enter only an ex-Grand Union pair. So we were down to four pairs. *Cairo* and *Warwick* could not enter, as Sonia Smith was a member of the Council.

The judging was to be done by Lord Lucan and myself, and it proved to be quite a difficult job. The S. E. Barlow and Samuel Barlow pairs both had a very casual approach and could hardly be seriously considered, which left only the Ovaltine and the D & IWE pairs. The Ovaltine boats were fully painted in the traditional style; the D & IWE pair had their new, non-traditional livery of blue and yellow. An additional factor we had to take into account was the fact that it was fairly general knowledge that Alf Best (skipper of the D & IWE pair) had asked to come and work for me. After much heart searching, the cup was awarded to the Ovaltine pair *Mimas* and *Ray*, with *Alton* and *Ayr* as the runners-up.

Kenelm returning from the IWA rally at Market Harborough in 1950, with Tom Foxon steering into The Boot lock, Lapworth, on the Stratford Canal.

During the rally, both *Kenelm* and *Columba* got involved in running trips for the spectators along the arm. Also, one afternoon, *Kenelm* was used to carry the Dagenham Girl Pipers, who had been booked as part of the entertainment.

As the time went on, it was becoming increasingly obvious that things were hotting up between the rival factions of the IWA. As I saw it, the whole thing was so childish and unnecessary, and I was actually looking forward to the day when we could leave the rally. When that day came, we said goodbye and departed with very mixed feelings. I must say here and now that, as a result of what I had heard and learned at the rally, my feelings were tied even more firmly to the cause being put by what I considered to be the practical boating community, rather than what I came to think of as the "Arty and Crafty" Brigade. In fact, the divisions were never all that clear-cut. I had friends, for instance, who were firmly bonded to the practical boating side and yet were in support of the Chairman and his seemingly impractical policies.

However, the rally, in spite of the internal divisions, had been a success. It had firmly placed the canals of England on the map, and had demonstrated to government (both national and local) and to the D & IWE that there was a great recreational potential on the waterways.

Our own personal objective was to get back north as soon as possible. We called at Braunston to refuel and get provisions. Then we set off for Kingswood Junction.

Chapter Ten

DUNSTAN

In 1950, when I first knew it, it was possible to think of the Stratford-on-Avon Canal as two waterways, joined in the end-on connection at Kingswood Junction. The southern arm had a designed depth of 3 feet 3 inches, whereas the northern arm had 3 feet 6 inches designed depth and rather ampler dimensions all round. The canal had been started in 1793, and both arms were of approximately the same length. The two halves were to have very different fortunes. The lower half, connected to the River Avon at Stratford, soon deteriorated and was mainly an agricultural canal. The northern half, because it was slightly larger, took a longer time for the effects of silting to become a problem. The GWR took over the complete canal and within a few years of this, the southern half was virtually unusable. The northern half continued to be more or less navigable until about 1950. The main reason why the northern half fared better was because it was a handy short cut between the Grand Union and the Birmingham and Worcester Canals. Both were very prosperous waterways, but though used more than the southern half, the northern part did not get the traffic one might have expected.

For us, approaching it up the one furlong arm of the Grand Union, it was a useful road, but it was obvious that we were the first to have used the route for a very long time. We had considerable difficulty with the first lock. On *Kenelm* we had to take out the beams and tighten the chains. We had trouble almost all the way with weed, rubbish and lack of water. At Kings Norton Junction there was a wrestling match with the guillotine stop gate which we only just won.

At this point we turned into the Worcester and Birmingham, then went on past Cadbury's at Bournville, where *Columba* and *Uranus* had loaded chocolate crumb worth over £9,000 some eighteen months before. We went back to the northern canal at Middlewich, so that Bob and I could go down to Etruria to collect *Dunstan*.

I must confess that at this time we were beginning to have problems. It had seemed to be a good investment to purchase *Dunstan* and *Kenelm* whilst still retaining *Columba* and *Uranus*. There was no denying, however, that there were likely to be two major headaches, crews and cargoes, in the months ahead. The crew problem was greater up north, where I was still to a certain extent a stranger, than down on the Grand Union. But the other private companies were also having difficulties crewing their boats. These included Thomas Clayton and Cowburn and Cowpar, both operating on the Birmingham and Shropshire Union Canals. They, however, were both concerned solely with the carriage of tars and chemicals. They had regular runs and were highly specialised. The Mersey, Weaver and Ship Canal Carrying Company and the Anderton Company operated almost exclusively on the Trent and Mersey. They too had regular runs.

We collected *Dunstan* and were very proud of her, as she was a fine-looking boat. I was hoping she would be the first of a new kind of modern canal boat. Mersey Weaver had carried out my instructions to the letter and/ *Dunstan* was now completely flush-decked, with the exception of the shortened mast-box and this was fitted with the usual telescopic mast. We arrived at Preston Brook with *Columba* and were given orders. Our first job with *Dunstan* was not what I would have chosen for a first trial of her capabilities. We were to go down the Anderton Boat Lift to load from a lighter on the River Weaver. This unfortunately meant that there was no available space on the lighter to put all *Dunstan*'s hatch covers, so the loading turned out to be something of a disaster. Had this first loading taken place at a wharf, we could have adapted later for loading in different conditions. The one bright feature was that it was not raining. We did load the cargo of tomato purée in due course, but it had been awkward to get safely stowed and left a feeling, on both sides, that we had been somewhat inefficient.

Shortly after this I went down to London on one of my routine visits home. These visits had become rather more infrequent than when I was working on the Grand Union. On this occasion Gerry Bird, who had often travelled with me, got in touch to tell me of a friend of his in the Potteries. He wanted a new motor boat and asked if I knew of one for sale. This started a maggot burrowing in my brain. Gerry said the firm, John Walley, had only one boat and it was becoming worn out. I had a warm corner in my heart for *Dunstan*, but we had difficulties in working and crewing her and it really would make much more sense to let her go. The outcome was that after heart-searching, I sold *Dunstan*. I felt sure that had I been able to work her myself, I could have made a success of it and she would have had a rosy future with me. But, as things stood, selling was really the only solution. We did

Gerry Bird steering *Columba* on the Grand Union

one more salt trip and, once again, after the exigencies of the first one, it seemed rather routine and dull without difficulties and dangers. This time, we did not go on the Kennet & Avon but discharged into lorries at Caversham Lock in Reading.

There was one rather unusual incident. Just as we were leaving Osney Lock, Oxford, we had a rather hurried exchange with the lock-keeper. This was a lady lock-keeper (unusual then in what tended to be a man's world), who had been appointed since our last trip. She called out, "Be careful of the wires below Sandford Lock". Canal people, whether through lack of schooling or some other reason, always pronounce the word "weir" as "wier" or "wire". I could not think of what this warning could mean, unless the Thames Conservancy Board were fitting new weirs to release the flood water, and the work might cause some obstruction. So this was what I was looking out for. Whilst there was still no sign of any work of this kind, Bob suddenly called out, "Mind the wires!". At the last moment, I saw one of the wires in question as it caught round our mast, funnel and chimney. There were two strands of wire about a hundred yards apart and hanging down low from poles and strung across the river. They were almost invisible. They were used for measuring the flow of the river. Although we struck them, we were lucky not to break either of them.

This was the last of the salt runs, in part due to the closing of the Kennet & Avon Canal. But our other problem was that we could bring so much salt in one load that no more was required for a very long period, so our very success meant that our journeys could not be frequent enough to keep us occupied.

On this third trip we had good weather and we made the run in 10 days. This time, after unloading we did not go downstream, but returned north via Oxford, engaged in some towing. John Gould had taken delivery of two old buttys which he had purchased from Harvey-Taylor of Aylesbury. With John and some additional lads from Newbury, we took them from Reading to Birmingham, where they were to be docked. We dropped them off at the Spencer Abbott yard and continued up north.

We had several loadings between the north and Birmingham before disaster struck. *Kenelm*'s engine failed. We carried on for a few more weeks with *Columba*, but by now there were other problems. We were over-manned. Perhaps because of this we got rather short of temper. Loadings were bad,Tom left, and joined up with Ray White who, like Tom, had come to me from IWA. They operated a motor belonging to the North-Western Division called *Eagle*. The partnership was short-termed, because Tom was called for National Service in the RAF, of which more later.

With Bob left, we went back to operating *Columba* and *Uranus* as a pair. But things were not going all that well. It was doubly unfortunate that we were not doing further salt runs as Bob, with his home in Newbury, found that affairs there required him to visit from time to time and this could not be fitted in to a cargo run, so Bob had to take time off to be able to go home periodically.

Columba's engine was giving trouble at intervals. I decided that after discharging our next cargo, overhaul was obviously necessary. Les Allen, then the foreman who had been at Spencer Abbott when the boats were docked in 1949, had now set up his own yard. I thought that it would be worthwhile to take *Columba* and *Uranus* to his yard at Oldbury on the BCN. The problem was finding a suitable engine as at this time, marine engines of the correct capacity and at reasonable cost were very scarce. When we arrived, Bob left me and returned to Newbury.

We were now in the spring of 1951 and this is an opportune time to backtrack to cover other events. The major of these, of course, was the crisis in the IWA.

Since the Market Harborough Rally, things had deteriorated, both rapidly and seriously. The IWA seemed to have divided into two groups, each with completely different ideas about how the organisation should develop. There was no doubt that the more reasoned faction was what could perhaps be called the rebels. The other more extreme and hysterical party was led by Chairman, Robert Aickman. The unwilling champion of the rebels was the Secretary, Tom Rolt. In the following account, I have tried to set out as fairly as possible the opposing attitudes, even though at times I was classed firmly among the rebels.

Things came to a head at the next meeting of the Council after the rally, at which it was decided to call a General Meeting at the Holborn Restaurant in London, which I attended with my mother. As the meeting progressed, it was obvious that the Chairman and his associates were determined that heads would roll. It was painful to see my mother's mounting distress as the possibility increased that many of our friends would be thrown out. There was little that the thinking members of the Council could do. A spiteful, badly-worded no-compromise resolution was put to the meeting; it was obvious that the Chairman was determined that it should go through (which it did), and that the result would be that many people who opposed him, including Tom Rolt, Sonia Smith and myself, would be thrown out. In the event, not only these three, but S. E. Barlow, Gerry Bird, John Gould, Charles Hadfield, W.B. Hatherley, John Lester, Lord Lucan and Angela Rolt were also to go.

The result of all this was to hold back the IWA for several years; until in fact, the removal of Robert Aickman as Chairman. At the beginning, everyone respected Aickman for his drive and enthusiasm, even if some of his policies were suspect. The actual motion which caused the final crisis was this:

> "This Council confirms the policy of the Association is to advocate the restoration to good order, and maintenance in good order, of every navigable waterway; and the fullest use of every navigable waterway by both commercial and pleasure traffic."

The word that exercised us all at the time was "every" - looking back I think we should have concerned ourselves more exactly with what was meant in the motion by "navigable".

For my part, I was horrified on several grounds. Who was to pay for it all? (It would obviously cost perhaps several hundreds of millions of pounds to carry out.) Who was to own these renovated waterways? The big question was, what was a navigable waterway? From the attitude of the Council it would seem that they meant every canal that had ever been constructed, no matter what its present condition. Did they really mean this policy to apply to the Thames & Severn Canal or the Wey & Arun Canal, for instance, of which there was by then little visible sign and would therefore in effect mean building the canal all over again, as if for the first time *[it is interesting to note that both these canals are currently being restored, albeit slowly]*.

I felt that the net result of all this would be that the Association would become a laughing stock as far as the Docks and Inland Waterways Executive was concerned. This would apply equally to the National Association of Inland Waterway Carriers and the various navigable river authorities, let alone any canal carriers who got to hear of the proposals.

The really disturbing aspect of the whole affair, however, was the intolerance shown to any ideas differing from those of the Chairman. It seemed to be fundamental to him that if anyone did not subscribe utterly to his views, and especially to the proposals in that one resolution, out he went. Even those who had done and were doing highly important work on the various committees were not safe.

Take, for instance, the committee with which I was most closely associated, the Small Working Boat Sub-Committee. Its members were Tom Rolt, Lord Lucan, Sonia Smith, Lewis Edwards and myself. There were six major projects on which we were working at the time. There was the "Blue and Yellow" campaign, a project on the schooling of children of boatmen, co-operation with Trade Unions, discussions about the improvement of rates of pay, and exploring the possibilities of improving facilities for loading and unloading - all vital to the continuance of the working boatmen on the waterways. After the fracas, the only member of the sub-committee left was Lewis Edwards!

I think all the six things on which we were working were more important than the useless attempts to stretch what little money was available into projects for the possible restoration of long since defunct and dry waterways. It may well be that this is a major reason why there are virtually no working boats on the canal today. I felt that it was more important to preserve the network of canals as they were at that time and to retain our credibility.

A memorandum had been circulated giving the views of a number of the rebel members of the IWA regarding the disputed motion, and signed quite openly by them. This was criticising Caesar indeed. At Robert Aickman's instance, a motion was passed which, in the words of the Minute Book, asked for the "recantation and apology" of those who had signed - in writing. Lord Lucan resigned. Most of the others ignored the request to apologise, with the result that Gerry Bird, John Gould, Charles Hadfield, W.B. Hatherley, John Lester, Tom Rolt, Angela Rolt, Sonia Smith and myself were all asked to resign from the IWA.

Looking back on these events after a period of nearly 50 years it is, I suspect, difficult to be objective. In those days I did not seem to differentiate between broad (14 feet) and narrow (7 feet) canals, as I do today. I was not thinking of the present-day commercial canals, largely because it was virtually impossible to get to them from the south and east. The network I was mainly considering was the system radiating from Birmingham. It was this above all that I wanted to be preserved and which I viewed as being the main concern of the IWA. Outside of these canals were stretches of both broad and narrow canals which had fallen into disrepair and become neglected or semi-abandoned. These waterways were really a part of the network and their restoration would enhance the whole system.

There were certain broad waterways, not part of the network, which I felt could once again form important arteries of commerce if properly handled. These included the Stroudwater, the Thames & Severn, the Kennet and Avon and even the Wey & Arun Canal. I was doubtful whether to include the Basingstoke Canal in this group, as it did not seem to go anywhere.

Lastly was my third group, waterways already badly neglected and which seemed unlikely to serve any useful purpose in the future. They were isolated and so could not get the helping hand of a healthy neighbour. The group included the Chesterfield Canal, the Chard Canal, the Crewkerne Canal, the Bridgewater & Taunton and the Grand Western Canals.

I trust that in this discussion of the crisis in the affairs of the IWA I shall not be accused of raking the coals once more. These events of 1950 and 1951 were of the greatest importance to me, and to be deprived of participation in, particularly, the Working Boat Sub-Committee made a considerable difference to my working life. To have omitted to mention the contretemps and its outcome would have been impossible and a distortion of the facts.

Chapter Eleven

ENGINE PROBLEMS

All in all it seemed that I was going to be in for a pretty worrying time. Whilst I was in the Mediterranean during the war, my mother had been operated on for cancer. Now she was unwell again. It looked very much as if there was going to be a repetition of her illness. Added to this there was also the problem of *Columba*'s engine.

I might have been able to get a replacement - another National - from Bulls Bridge, but I had been away from there for so long that I was out of touch with events and did not feel that I could suddenly go back and solicit favours. In any case, I was beginning to wonder, in view of their age (15 years or more) whether a National engine would be a good investment. It would be more sensible to have a new engine. But it was only four or five years after the end of the war, and engine manufacture and delivery were not back in full swing. The field for canal boat engines was so restricted that very few firms were doing any construction or development work. Nor could anyone promise a reasonable delivery date. As usual, whenever you want something the day before yesterday, there is nothing available. I would have liked a Russell Newbery engine, but they too were unable to supply. There was an engine available from Fowlers which was a good, slow-moving four-stroke single-cylinder diesel similar to that used in the Field Marshall tractor. Unfortunately, there was no marine gear-box being manufactured, so that was out. Similarly, Rolls Royce had recently taken over Sentinel. Again, there was no gear-box, and no likelihood of one in the near future.

One fateful day I was in Victoria Street in London and happened to glance at the door of some offices. The sign on the brass plate said, "The Bolinder Company". I went in and up the stairs and was greeted by Mr Wade, Bolinder's chief salesman in England. He explained that he was also their chief engineer, so I told him of my problems. Much to my surprise and joy he informed me that he could supply me.

The engine I was offered was a semi-diesel, light-weight, compact, high-speed twin with integral gear-box. It produced 20 horse-power at one thousand revolutions per minute with two-to-one reduction gear. The cost was £250. It seemed to be the answer to all my prayers.

Mr Wade explained to me that the engine was started by a blowlamp and compressed air (the blowlamp also operated on compressed air). He said that delivery could take place almost immediately. All that was required was to select a yard in which the work could be done, to sign the contract and pay the money. On this last count, the family (in the person of my grandmother) was assisting once more.

Part of my surprise at all this was that I was used to Bolinder producing big, old-style, single-cylinder semi-diesels, and had no idea that they were now turning out engines of the kind that I was being offered. Mr Wade told me that the twin had been developed for fishing boats and they were sure from many years of experience with canal craft that it would be entirely suitable for my purpose, too.

Alas, I was not to know at the time that the engine carried within its sleek exterior the seeds of problems ahead.

I got in touch with Les Allen; *Columba* was towed to Oldbury and work started on preparing the engine-hole. In due course the engine arrived. It was certainly very compact, taking up only about two-thirds of the space required for the National. It was also much lower. On going into the engine-hole the humorist might be excused for wondering where the engine was. There was a blowlamp attached to one side and operating through the cowling between the two cylinders. In addition, there was a compressed air cylinder about the size of a five gallon oil drum, which had to be fixed to the side of the engine-hole.

The engine was started initially by detaching the integral blowlamp and using an ordinary paraffin lamp. A retractable peg was pulled out of the fly-wheel when the correct temperature had been reached. The peg was then stepped on, the fly-wheel turned and Voila! The engine started and as it did so, automatically began to recharge the compressed air cylinder. The temporary blowlamp was removed, the engine stopped, the proper blowlamp connected and filled with diesel. Next the compressed air was turned on, the blowlamp lit and, when the temperature was correct, the compressed air valve operated to blow air into the cylinders. Now the engine should start! We began to get trouble early on; It was easy to waste compressed air on the blowlamp. This was caused by not gauging the temperature correctly. It was probably safer to use the starting peg. But there were times when this was also unsatisfactory.

The fact was, of course, that the demands on an engine for canal work were different from those of a fishing boat. When fishing, the engine was not being continually put into and out of gear (as we needed to do in locks) so the engine remained at a constant temperature for several hours at a time. Once we had got used to the engine we went out on trials. It was fortunate that Bob was still with me at this time. Although we had these problems, there was nothing that we thought we would be unable to manage with patience and experience.

When we were at Oldbury, also in the yard was a most charming and interesting family called Lehmann. Mr Lehmann was a Belgian Jew who had been most shamefully treated during the German occupation, as a result of which he was now a very sick man. A few years later, after I was married, we became great friends and my wife, Martin, and I used to visit them in their house in Tettenhall Road in Wolverhampton. Unfortunately in due course we lost touch with this very nice family. In the Oldbury yard he was converting an old wooden narrow boat, with Les Allen's help, making it into a house-boat for himself. He was probably inspired by reading Tom Rolt's *Narrow Boat*.

At this time the toy manufacturer, Mobo, was producing a kind of pedal car called "The Snail". This was shaped like a huge snail and was stamped out in two halves which were joined together by a seat. Mr Lehmann persuaded the firm to stamp him out two halves in brass (they were each about two feet in diameter) to attach to either side of the boat's cabin. Kept highly polished, they ensured that no-one could be unaware that the narrow boat, also, was called *Snail*.

When the time came to leave Oldbury, we returned to the northern road. At about this time I received a letter from another enthusiast who wanted to come and work on the boat. A few days before he was due to arrive, Bob had an urgent summons to return to Newbury because of family problems. So I was alone» with the boats at Etruria whilst waiting for the new chap to arrive. I felt it would be good to have a crew of three again. Unfortunately, from almost the moment of his appearance, he began to show that he was temperamentally unsuitable for work on the canal boats. I do not remember much about him - I know he was somewhere in my age bracket, between 38 and 45. We killed a little time going on some training runs. I had to come to the Potteries to collect *Uranus*, left here at the end of the last salt run, but there was no possibility of work from there that I could find. The temperamental unsoundness of my new man was not helped by the idiosyncrasies of the new engine, which was proving to be most unreliable. It would not tick over in locks, it got cold and had to be restarted, which entailed using the blowlamp again. Sometimes it would start on the air cylinder, or on a kick-start, but very often it would not start at all. Then it was necessary to dismantle the blowlamp, a tedious business as the engine cowling had to be removed and without it there was no way of concentrating the heat. As there was no way of fixing or even standing the blowlamp, it had to be hand-held the whole time, so nothing else could be attended to at the same time. All this was no help and in due course the new fellow left.

So there I was, feeling rather deflated and sorry for myself, tied up on the main line at Etruria and wondering how I was going to solve my triple problem of no crew, a difficult engine and no cargo. One day I spotted a Josher pair. As they passed we exchanged the usual greetings, then, I suppose realising that I was alone, the skipper asked, "Are you wanting a mate?". I replied with alacrity, "Yes, I am." "We can get you one - a real boatman, young and keen." Sure enough, about four days later the young boatman arrived. His name was Don Rosenburg.

Don had been working an ex-Severn and Canal Carrying Company boat called *Ash*. The S & CCC's fleet had been absorbed into the BW Northern fleet on nationalisation. They were strange craft, built like a biscuit tin, with all welded hulls. They were built of thin plate, with little internal structure and so were largely corrugated for strength. They had virtually no tumble home at the bows. Also, the engine-hole was right aft with the boatman's cabin forward of it. This was not the most satisfactory arrangement for comfortable living. It was awkward for cooking between locks and for looking after the cabin stove and so forth. Fortunately, the counter was of steel, for if it had been wooden as usual, it would have been difficult to keep it clean and free of oil. I could not understand how this design had originated. It was a strange arrangement, and I could only think that it must have been produced by somebody without much knowledge of working boats.

Don and I got on well together from the very start. He had had a problem with the law - I forget exactly what; either poaching or using a shot-gun without a licence or something like that. Anyhow, he had to appear in the court, so the day of his arrival we set off for the court in Crewe. On my good recognizance he was put on probation for quite a short period. This was very fortunate, because as far as I was concerned he was ideal as a boatman. His expertise otherwise as a poacher was no concern of mine.

Once the case was over, we returned to Top Lock, Etruria, where *Columba* and *Uranus* were still moored. In view of Don's experience and willingness to work, I decided to return to the Grand Union. Two days later we set off south and took a somewhat leisurely run down.

We tied up at Kings' Langley, and I rang home to enquire about my mother. I found that she was very much worse, so accelerated my progress and arrived at Bulls Bridge about a week after our departure from Etruria. From here it was comparatively easy to get home, but also had the advantage that I could get the latest information about loadings. As luck would have it, there were quite a few boats waiting for orders, which in my present situation was encouraging. It did not necessarily suit Don as well as it did me. We had both been getting more and more frustrated by the Bolinder. On long pounds and with few locks, the engine went like a dream and rarely stalled. But on short pounds with more locks was where the problem began. The engine had not been designed to idle and in the situation the compressed air cylinder quickly ran out. We felt that the cylinder really was not large enough. After some time, I came to the conclusion that a more sensible arrangement would have been to use compressed air solely for heating, but to have an electric starter to actually start the engine when the temperature was right.

The end came at Bulbourne, at the northern end of the Tring summit. I remember quite well that it was the Thursday before Easter. We were loaded and going north and had planned to tie up at the bottom of "Maffers" (the boatman's version of Marsworth) for the holiday period. Our frustration had grown and grown as we climbed the heavily-locked section of the Grand Union to Cowroast, our engine continually cutting out, and losing locks to let other pairs through. We fiddled with and cursed what had now become "that bloody engine". I suppose it was not surprising that we finally exploded. The inevitable result was that Don left. It was all rather a pity, looking back, for Don was a good and likable boatman and companion. When we were not overwhelmed by the Bolinder, we got on well together.

Soon after Don left, Alf Best appeared with his boats and family. He had some two years before suggested to me that he would be willing to come and work for me if ever I wanted a boat captain. So, on that fateful Thursday, Alf was on his way to Brum and gave a helping hand down the Marsworth flight.

1951 - *Kenelm* and *Uranus* below "Maffers", Wally steering.
Alf Best about to get off at bridge 'ole with bike.

Nothing could be done about the engine, so the load had to be bow-hauled. By evening we were down at the bottom and tied up. Alf left me there and pressed on to try and clear Stoke Bruerne before the holiday, with the parting assurance that he would find me a crew. I have always been heartened and a little astonished by the willingness of the majority of the boat people to help out when you were down on your luck, as I most certainly was now. Canal boating in the old style always seemed to be governed by the example of the Good Samaritan. It did not seem to matter if the problem was a little one or a big one; sheeting-up a perishable cargo like sugar or grain on the sudden coming of a downpour of rain; starting up a recalcitrant engine, even dismantling and rebuilding it; help through a lock if you were short-handed; the lifting of a paddle; the closing of a lock gate; all done with good humour and friendliness.

Then there was the friendly chat when another captain jumped on your counter as you gave him a lift to the next lock. There was always a friendly wave from the captain of a passing pair and an exchange of useful information: that the locks were all ready to the top of the next flight; to warn you that you only had one ready because a two-handed pair had passed them just above the next lock; occasionally, who had just had an addition, or married, or died.

I shall never forget young Jim Peaseland in a typical example of canal people helping each other out. This was some months after I had been married and Martin was working the pair with me. I had gone on ahead on the bike to get the locks below Maffers ready, and in a strong wind across the flats, Martin was having trouble managing the breasted-up boats. Jim, then aged 12, passing on his father's boats, spotted her difficulties. jumped niftily onto *Columba*'s counter and with a polite, "Let me have 'em, Missus", took her safely into the lock.

Don's sudden departure was to change my whole life.

Chapter Twelve

MARRIAGE

I got back that Easter weekend feeling rather depressed and unhappy. My mother had been invited to go and stay with some old friends in Woking. I took a day off to go down and see her; she was not at all well, very flushed, unsteady on her feet and tending to put on weight. I found it terribly sad,especially as nobody appeared to have any idea as to what the trouble was.

Two days later, back with the boats still loaded and tied up at the bottom of Maffers, I spotted a pair of Grand Union boats going south. They slowed down as they passed and off stepped a young man of about 17. He came across to me. "Mr Knill? I'm your new steerer."

Was I pleased to see him! He introduced himself as Wally James. He was a typical product of a boat family, unable to read or write and, as with all youngsters of the time, he faced having to complete two years National Service at the age of 18 (There was a little doubt, as he may have been considered unsuitable because of his illiteracy). However, he had a year's grace and he wished to fill this working for me. Wally was a very good steerer and I can see him even now, sitting on the cabin roof, feet dangling in the hatches, as he took *Columba* round the most intricate turns with no trouble at all.

The next day, we resumed our interrupted journey north. The delay had in no way inconvenienced the firm for whom the cargo was destined. It was part of a large shipment which had required many pairs to complete. As with a lot of canal traffic, such as coal and other cargoes from the docks, time in transit was not important. The requirement was that there should be a continuous chain of deliveries, rather like a sausage machine.

We still had trouble from our recalcitrant engine. The first day, it seemed that all was going to be well again. We got to Bradwell after working 13 locks with the intention of tying up at Cosgrove. But it was not to be. We lost all power and could do nothing but tie up, motor ahead and butty astern, and send for assistance from Bolinders. They sent a new, young engineer. He could not understand what had happened, but took the gear-box to pieces.

Then came a series of Bolinder chaps, whilst we got more and more frustrated as they came and went. Altogether, we were stuck there for six weeks. It was indeed fortunate that the D & IWE did not seek to transfer the load to another pair of boats. This breakdown, infuriating as it was, was destined to change my whole life, as you will see.

One of the things on the credit side of the six weeks stuck here at Bradwell was that it gave me every opportunity to go down to London to visit my mother. By good fortune, the point at which we were tied up was on the outskirts of Bradwell and there could have been much worse places to be. We were only three-quarters of a mile south from Wolverton Station, on the main line to Euston. In fact in those halcyon days, there was even a station at Bradwell itself, as it was on the branch line to Newport Pagnell.

By now my mother had been moved to St Thomas's Hospital. We had still not been told what the trouble was. I arrived at the hospital one afternoon to find another visitor sitting by my mother's bed. This visitor was one Martin Barnes, whom I had not seen or thought about since she had been a guest at my 21st Birthday party some 16 years before. My mother at once started a match-making process. In due course this "campaign" was sufficiently successful for me to ask Martin to come and spend her summer holidays on the boats, even though we were still immobilised at Bradwell. There always seemed to be hope that the hold-up would not last any longer.

A wedding photograph posed for the press. Martin is performing mystical rites with the tiller - we were tied up at the time! I am in another world, nursing Bosun.

When I arrived back and told Wally, he was ecstatic and immediately went into a match-making routine of his own. The result was that I was under attack from two fronts at once. I must say that I was beginning to warm to Martin myself. She was about two years older than me, mad keen on boats of all kinds and used to roughing it. She had been in the Guide movement since the age of 10, was a Sea Ranger and had recently been the leader of a relief team in the Guide International Service in Holland, Germany and Denmark.

Once again it proved lucky that we had three cabins on *Uranus* and *Columba*. We cleared out the butty cabin for Martin to sleep there, but still used it for cooking and eating. The 10 or 14 days of Martin's holiday proved to be successful. (Martin's amusing account of this time appears at the end of the book.) Not only did Bolinders manage to repair the gear-box and get us under way again, I also asked Martin to marry me. She accepted right away and we both agreed that we did not want a long engagement. We tentatively fixed a day in November (it was now August), a decision that was also influenced by my mother's illness.

Martin had been a friend of my mother's for at least 16 years, and she admitted to me (after we were married) that when she had first met me at my 21st Birthday party she thought me rather dull. Perhaps the time I had spent in the Navy had wrought a change. We always used to joke that Martin had married me for my boats and I for her flat in Chelsea. Whatever it was, we had a very happy marriage. Of course we had our ups and downs, but I think we had 33 very good years together. I know it brought me out.

At the end of her stay I took Martin to Wolverton Station and said goodbye. I think Wally was nearly as sorry as I was to see her go. They were then, and remained, very good friends.

To move from the sublime to the ridiculous, I must mention one incident of moment that occurred at Bradwell. In the builder's yard we discovered a magnificent mahogany horse-collar (in other words, a lavatory seat) which we purchased for 10 shillings (50p). Bolted to the steel engine room bulkhead and with a clip to keep it folded up when not in use, it looked superb and was eminently comfortable. Gone were the days of bright red circles around our buttocks.

We carried on the rest of summer, slowly mastering the "bloody Bolinder". This did not, however, mean that there were no problems with it. We got quite adept at whipping off the casing to be able to use an ordinary blowlamp when we were out of compressed air.

Having Wally as my steerer introduced me to a completely new set of friends amongst the boaters. It was at about this time that a young "captain" came up to me on a lock side somewhere on the "Junction" and spoke to me.

"Mr Knill? I've been thinking about making a change and wondered if there's any chance of coming to work for you? The name's Wilson, Ron Wilson."

"Well, Ron, I'd be delighted to have you, but there's not much chance at the present. I expect you know Alf Best?"

"Yes, I do, Mr Knill."

"He's already asked me for a job and I've promised him that as soon as I need a captain, he should have the first pair."

"Fair enough."

"But I will certainly remember you, Ron, and if I put on another pair, the job's yours."

"Can't say fairer than that, Gaffer. I hope you didn't mind me asking?"

The upshot of this conversation was that when I went ashore, Ron came to work for me and a splendid captain he was. Without exaggeration, I do not think I have ever come across such loyalty as I got from Ron. Soon after he came to work for me he lost his youngest child, and Martin was able to help with the funeral arrangements. We still write to and telephone each other, mainly at Christmas. But there is rather a charming sequel. Ron, who has left the cut now, has had a boat built for himself and he had named it *Kenelm*, after the motor boat which he captained for me and which he worked with the butty *Uranus*. By a further strange coincidence, immediately after the launching of his own *Kenelm*, the first boat to go by was *Uranus*, now converted from a butty boat to a motor boat.

The wedding was firmly settled for 5th November, 1951, and we arranged to have a honeymoon of just a week. We decided that whilst we were away, we would have the forward cabin on *Columba* tarted up a bit, and were lucky enough to be able to arrange for the work to be done by the old Fellows Morton yard at Uxbridge, which was the most convenient place for getting down to London. The ceremony was to take place at the Church of the Sacred Heart in Wimbledon and to be performed by one of my Grandfather's old chaplains, Father McCauley. The reception was to be at Martin's brother's flat in Chester Square, Chelsea. It was a fairly small affair. Wally, of course, was invited. There were lots of presents, including a fantastic number of mugs - think the word had got round about the boatman's tea-drinking propensities!

A doctor friend of Martin's lent her a car, and once the reception was over we set off for Alfriston in Sussex. It was for some reason considered safer for me to drive. So came about another great change in my circumstances. The next time we loaded, we would be three-handed.

Chapter Thirteen

A CHANGE OF ENGINE

The week of our honeymoon passed all too quickly. We had taken Bosun with us and he was unwittingly the cause of an amusing incident. During the second or third night, Martin was woken by me beating her and shouting in my sleep, "Bosun, get down!" It took me a good time to live that down.

It was mid-November when we got back to the boats. One reason for waiting this long was that my mother's condition had begun to deteriorate again and we were all beginning to fear the worst. It was particularly distressing for my grandmother, now in her late eighties, and due to go on for another three or four years yet. We had to consider seriously the possibility of having to sell the house in Wimbledon. We stayed in Martin's flat for this time, visiting my mother daily.

The first week back we spent at Uxbridge, to enable all the re-arrangements that my marriage had made necessary to be carried out.

Internally both *Columba* and *Uranus* were fine (except for that damned engine!) but external appearances were not too good. There had been such a rush since Martin had come to Bradwell for her holiday that it had not been possible to do anything about the paintwork, and for a while at least we decided to leave it that way.

Also during this week, we had a visit from the press, who took some good photographs. Perhaps I should say that the photographs were too good, since they showed up all the boat's blemishes only too well. There was one shot in particular in which I was holding Bosun whilst, Martin, standing by me, performed strange rites with the tiller - strange, since we were both breasted up and moored at the time.

Martin, with Bosun

Once we were back at work, we decided to go straight up to the coalfields, there being no cargoes northward from Limehouse or Brentford at the time. We had a couple of days to wait, so Martin and I went off to Birmingham, leaving Wally in charge.

We were nearing the end of the month, the weather was getting colder and there was the probability of ice. Sure enough, when we arrived at Stoke Bruerne it was to a very chilly spell, with ice forming on the canal and the prospect of snow. As we were to be here for a day or two, I took Martin along to meet Sister Mary. They got on very well and became firm friends.

Thanks to the transport policy of the new government, it was beginning to be increasingly difficult to get loadings northwards, and chances of loading for Birmingham or Northampton with grain were becoming few and far between. For a while, all our work was carrying coal from the Warwick coalfield, except for a couple of loads of grain for Northampton.

All this while we were having the same spasmodic trouble with the engine. It was fairly obvious that we must install a new engine, so I began to stir myself once more to find out if the supply situation had improved. One option I considered was a four-cylinder David Brown tractor engine, but I was not over enthusiastic about the idea, mainly because it was a comparatively new engine and because I distrusted it on account of it running at what I considered then to be a rather high rev-count.

In these days when we are so used to multi-cylinder, high-revving engines, it must be remembered that canal boats had always used slow or medium-speed engines. The Bolinder single cylinder, and the Petter, its English counterpart, at 500 revolutions per minute, were typical of the engines in normal use. Even the National, at 1,000 revs per minute, was regarded when it first came out with suspicion. These attitudes tend to die hard. It would be quite a leap in the dark to change from even the National with its two-to-one gear-box to a David Brown or a Thorneycroft with twice as many revs.

Then I had a bright idea. When I first started boating, I had bought a manual on diesel engines and looking through it once more I noticed that amongst others it dealt with the Widdop engine, one I had not considered before for several reasons. It was fairly low-speed, about 500 revs, and I thought that as with the Bolinder, there would be a lot of vibration. Also it seemed too large to fit into the engine-hole. Now I met someone who swore by them and told me they were much used on the Leeds and Liverpool Canal. They were made, I seem to remember, at either Runcorn or Stockport. This all sounded encouraging, so I went up to have a look. But disappointment prevailed when I got to the works, where I was told that I was about three months too late. The firm had been taken over by Brush, who had decided to discontinue production of the single-cylinder engine I had been hoping to purchase. This was part of their policy to cut out the making of all small engines and to concentrate on ships' engines. They did, however, inform me that now they were part of the Brush Group, they were advising customers to use the engine manufactured by Petter, which was also part of the Group. So, back to Braunston I trekked, then on down to Staines, hoping that they would have something for my needs.

Petters were most helpful and gave me all the information I needed about their small engines. There were four versions, 10 hp, 20 hp, 30 hp and 40 hp, all running at about 1,200 rpm with two-to-one reduction gears. It seemed to me that the 30 hp model was the one to consider. I made what was, I suppose, a fairly momentous decision - install a Petter three-cylinder engine.

It was a beautiful-looking engine, with enough copper piping to satisfy any boatman's heart. It was also painted a lovely pale green. Taken all in all, it was a leap in a the dark. I need not have worried. *Columba* was taken to Braunston, where Barlows removed the troublesome Bolinder (and sold it for me) and installed the new engine. Petters sent down their experts for trials, which went off fine, *Columba* was now one of a select few boats which had a three-cylinder engine. The others all belonged to the Samuel Barlow Coal Company, which had installed Gardner and Ruston engines.

The benefits of the new engine were soon obvious. It was not necessary to "flog" the engine, as we had had to do with the Bolinder (and to a lesser extent with the National). This resulted in smaller fuel consumption and less wear and tear, and the advantage that the engine had just that little bit extra when you needed it.

Columba - New Petter engine trials. Le Cheminant, Barlow's boat dock manager, with cap, stands beyond the funnel. John Hemelryk is in shirt sleeves. Others are believed to be Petter engineers.

Chapter Fourteen

GOING ASHORE

Now that we were working three-handed, life became much more relaxed, even when we were working hard to achieve good working times. From my earliest days as a Number One, I had always received the help and co-operation of the old established boatmen, and as Martin got on so very well with them, this bond was, if anything, enhanced by her presence in the crew.

However, all was not well. There were signs that the canals were imperceptibly but definitely running down. At Brentford, Regent's Canal Dock or Limehouse, for instance, boats were tied up waiting for loading rather longer than they had been in the past. This longer waiting time was also repeated in the coal fields. The extra time involved may have been only half a day or a day at a time, but by the end of the month, this added up to an appreciable amount. The reasons were not far to seek, and were two-fold.

Firstly was the denationalisation and freeing of road transport by the Tory Government of 1950. This led to more canal traffic (and railway traffic, too, for that matter) being transferred to the roads. The almost immediate effect was to close down the buffer depots which were alongside canals and railways all over the country. The most important depots for canals were at Brentford, Tring, Blisworth, Northampton, Weedon and Tyseley, Sherborne Street, Sampson Road and Bordesley in Birmingham, and Stourport; which we had visited when working down the Staffordshire and Worcestershire Canal.

The second reason was the closing down of Fellows, Morton and Clayton, a firm which had been trading for at least 80 years and had built up a fantastic amount of goodwill during that time. They had been innovative in their handling of business. For instance, they had been the first to introduce steam haulage and later, first to install diesel engines on canals; their last steamer, *Viceroy*, was converted to diesel in 1927. Over the years they had acquired many customers and cargoes, some being unique to them. Two of their most famous clients were probably Typhoo Tea and HP Sauce.

When Fellows, Morton and Clayton ceased trading, their boats were all purchased by the British Waterways Board and added to their fleet in the Northern and Southern Divisions. BWB also took over their depots in London, Birmingham and the north. For some reason, however the Board did not get the trade as well as the boats, so their old amount of trade was now spread out much more thinly over the augmented fleet and their sub-contractors. By degrees the sub-contractors, who had served them so loyally since the end of the war, were dropped through sheer lack of cargoes. This debacle was reflected in the coal fields, too. We saw the unusual sight of ex-Fellows Morton boats carrying coal - something they had very rarely done before their take-over, as they usually had sufficient return loadings of other cargoes back from Birmingham to London and other points.

The effect of all this on my operations was that it seemed to me to be desirable to enlarge my fleet - which may seem a strange decision in view of the foregoing. We had decided that the way to survive was for us to get our own cargoes as soon as possible. We already had three boats - the two motors *Columba* and *Kenelm* and the butty *Uranus* - and it seemed reasonable to get another butty to increase possible loads without increasing the cost of carrying them. I knew I would have no difficulty in getting crews, as I had already had offers from both Alf Best and Ron Wilson and several others had spoken to me on the subject as well. In fact it was getting quite embarrassing turning down possible captains once the word had gone around that I was going for another pair. Although I was a comparative stranger to the canals, for some reason best known to them the canal people seemed to trust me.

On Martin's next visit to Sister Mary at Stoke Bruerne, it was confirmed that she was going to have a baby. So there now arose a degree of uncertainty about crewing for the next few months, or at least until I had a decision as to whether to go ashore or not.

Meanwhile my poor mother had been allowed to go home to live with my grandmother, but early in March 1952 her health deteriorated rapidly. She was moved again, this time to a home in Balham run by an Anglican order of nuns and known as the House of God. She finally passed away here on the feast of St Fidelis (April 24th), which has always seemed to me to be an appropriate date. We attended her funeral; she was buried in the churchyard of St Marie's, Rugby, one of the churches which the great Victorian architect, A. W. Pugin had designed.

By now, Wally was nearly 18 and like all lads of that age, he received his calling-up papers, so the time had come for us to think of parting company. With this and Martin's pregnancy we would soon be two crew members short and replacements were essential.

It was at this time, too, that Martin and I had made a decision to buy a house. We had often noticed on our travels that there was a house which belonged to a local farmer alongside the Top Lock at Braunston. This, although little more than a shell, was now for sale and we decided that in spite of the work needing doing on it, it would be well worth the £500 asking price. It was very conveniently situated, it had a small garden and a sizable "outhouse" which would be just right to turn into a workshop, garage and store for boat gear. The cost of the restoration was £1,400, but this meant that for a total of £1,900 we acquired a house with four rooms downstairs and four up. There was no bathroom, but as part of the restoration one bedroom was easily converted to this purpose, complete with lavatory.

Shortly after Wally had to leave, I was in Martin's Chelsea flat when I had a visit from someone I had not seen for nearly 30 years. This was an old school friend of mine called John Hemelryk, who had come to ask me if I had a vacancy on the boats. This was most fortuitous, as John would be most useful to tide me over the gap between Wally's departure and the time when we would be able to run two pairs with two experienced boatmen; the time when Martin ceased being a "Boatman" and became a "lady-in-waiting".

One of the last trips Martin did with the boats was in May 1952. We took *Columba* round to Oldbury to tow back *Kenelm*. She had been left in Les Allen's yard after her engine had broken down the previous year and had been lying there ever since. Also with us was a friend of Martin's, Betty Ballantine, who had been a member of Martin's team in the Guide International Service. The trip took about 10 days. We finished at Braunston, where *Kenelm* was to have a new engine fitted and her cabin repainted ready for Ron Wilson to take over. I had decided that the new livery should have a rich Oxford blue as its main colour; we had already tried this out for *Kenelm* and *Dunstan* when they had docked at Mersey Weaver in Etruria. As *Dunstan* had been sold, *Kenelm* was now the only boat sporting this blue, so I thought it was best to revert to the original colour - Ayres Coach Red, as made by Mason's of Derby.

Shortly after Martin's last trip, coming up to a bridge somewhere near Ricky, I saw a young airman waving us down. It turned out to be Tom Foxon on a week-end leave from his depot, which I think was at Uxbridge. He was quite willing to help us out whenever he could. He had only to make his way to the nearest canal and hail a pair of passing boats and the boatmen would be quite happy to pass on news of our whereabouts and say whether we were due to pass shortly. He could wait and pick us up, spend a day or two helping us, then get himself to the nearest railway station to return to Uxbridge. He would have a good week-end and we would have the great advantage of a full crew for a day or two. This continued for about four or five months and only stopped when Tom found himself posted to Egypt. In this way we got through until August, the month in which the baby was due.

There was still a decision to be made, however, on the question of acquiring a new butty. A friend of Martin's had agreed to put up the money, but there was a choice of buying a second-hand one or having a new one built. Although the D & IWE had plenty of boats available for disposal, these were sold at intervals by competitive tender, so this led to a number of uncertainties. You could not be sure of when the sales would occur, or whether you would be able to get the actual boat you wanted, or when she would be available. All in all, I decided that it would be best to go for a new boat, and the obvious choice was to have her built by Barlows at Braunston. Frank Nurser accepted the order and the keel was duly laid. This meant that both the new boat and the baby were due to be delivered in mid-August and it became

Lucy under construction at Nursers' yard in Braunston.

1951 - *Columba*, newly docked and painted by Dave Clark. Petter engine trials in progress.

something of a lottery as to which would be first! On August 23rd the baby was born, and the butty, to be named *Lucy* after my mother, was in the painting dock about to have her lettering done - so I was able to phone Dave Clark, whose brush was poised ready, to have the legend "John Knill and Son" added to the gleaming new paintwork. The son was soon to be christened Thomas John Pugin Bartholomew.

Tom had been born in the Princess Beatrice Hospital in London and had been delivered by caesarean section by none other than the Queen's gynaecologist, John Peel - and all on the National Health. By this time, not only the butty but the house was almost ready and in mid-September, the whole family, Martin, myself, Tom and Bosun, moved in.

Arrangements had been made for both Alf Best and Ron Wilson to come and work for me. I had intended to pair *Columba* and *Uranus* as before, and *Kenelm* with *Lucy*. This would have meant that each family would have a reasonable amount of accommodation in three cabins. Unfortunately, as Burns so rightly says, "The best laid schemes o'mice and men gang a-gley" - and so it happened now. Alf Best arrived first, but *Uranus* was not ready. He prevailed upon me to let him have *Lucy* paired with *Columba*, which meant that he had rather more space in the cabins than there was in the other pair, which would have to go to Ron Wilson. Ron Wilson had the bigger family, so was not best pleased at the way things worked out, and I had to use some diplomacy in dealing with the matter.

Meanwhile, Martin and I were settling down in The Locks, Top Lock, Braunston - a somewhat tautological address, but it did ensure that we got our post delivered. *Uranus* was finishing off her re-painting, as was *Kenelm*. *Kenelm* was also having a new engine fitted and once again I had chosen a Petter three-cylinder.

Now that I had a house with a secure, walled garden, I began to consider the possibility of installing my own storage tank for the boats. We had until now been re-fuelling at many points, the principle one being that at the *Greyhound Inn* at Hawkesbury Stop, where it was also possible to obtain a wide range of articles as well as food and fuel. It was also possible to fuel at Braunston,

1951. New butty *Lucy,* named after John Knill's mother, in the paint dock at Braunston. Painted by Dave Clark.

Blisworth, Bulbourne and the main BWB Depot at Bulls Bridge; at Hatton and at several points in Birmingham at the various BWB depots there. I always thought of the one at Hawkesbury as being the most conveniently situated.

Fuel, of course, was still rationed and the kind that we used was coloured pink to make its detection easy if it were illegally used for road haulage. Other legal users of pink fuel were farmers for their agricultural machines and manufacturers with diesel-driven stationary engines used for industrial purposes. It cost about one shilling and six pence (7½p) a gallon and was marketed under various proprietary names.

I came to the conclusion that it would be a decided advantage to buy in bulk for my own boats, so I had a 250 gallon tank put in for the purpose. It was placed inside the garden and was raised on two brick piers to give a greater fall and therefore a better flow. We laid an underground pipe to the canal, a distance of about 25 yards, and this had a flexible steel hose with a tap on it at the bottom end. There was also another cock on the tank outlet. Both the boat tanks and the supply tank had dip-sticks, so that it was easy to check the fuel position at any time. The only problem - and that is too strong a word for it - was that the 25 yard pipe had to be emptied each time, so that amount of oil had to be allowed for when filling the boats.

Now I had two working crews, another idea was mooted to try to boost our trading figures and would also help soothe the situation caused by letting Alf have *Lucy*. Ron suggested that a rather bigger butty to work with *Kenelm* would be a great advantage. So I looked round, and found that British Waterways had a steel butty named *Thea* which would just fill the bill. I duly purchased her, and had renamed her *Mathilda* and she was then taken on by Ron Wilson, much to his (and his family's) satisfaction. *Mathilda* continued as *Kenelm's* butty until I sold the boats to Barlows.

I was now for the first time in the situation of paying two boatmen to work my boats, rather than paying wages to a crew directly under me. The normal practice of other firms doing this was to pay their captain a price per ton carried, on a sliding scale according to the type of cargo on board. There was also an agreement about special payments if the boats were held up through no fault of their own. I thought this could on occasions be unfair to the boatmen and decided on a different system, similar to one I had used with my own crew. This was to pay a fixed basic weekly rate and to add a tonnage rate to this as well. In this way, my chaps knew that they would always have a minimum wage each week and not, as others sometimes did, have the possibility of having some weeks with no money coming in at all. Of course, this was open to abuse by unscrupulous steerers, but I knew my boatmen, Ron Wilson and Alf Best, and Laurence Grantham who took Alf's place towards the end of my trading, and I can say with pride that never at any time did any of them try to get something to which they were not entitled. The men wanted to work for me because they knew of my reputation for fair dealing and they felt it would be unworthy of them not to treat me fairly in return.

I must add, however, that this "quid pro quo" policy of the fairness was not confined to a few boatmen - there were very few steerers that I had come across during my time on the canal who would not be prepared to employ and trust in exactly the same way as Ron, Alf and Laurence. My memory may have played me false, but I am fairly sure that the steerer's weekly wage was £14 and that the tonnage rate varied from one and sixpence to two shillings (7½p to 10p) a ton.

This system of payment turned out to be my downfall, as you will see. But, in all fairness to my crews, I do not see what else I could have done. I was very confident, I had probably the best captains available and four well-founded boats. The two motors boats had new engines and all were covered by insurance and against breakdown. What *could* go wrong?

Everything now seemed set fair. Aware of the diminishing traditional cargoes, I decided to address this by starting an advertising campaign. I reckoned that with my two pairs I could carry rather more than 100 tons of cargo per week.

At this time there were still around some copies of a book published by the Grand Union Canal Carrying Company which had first appeared in 1935. This had useful maps showing the position of every canal-side business between the junction of the Grand Union with the River Lee in East London and Birmingham.

I produced a printed illustrated leaflet, and copies were distributed to every firm shown on the maps, well not every one, as during the 15 years since publication some businesses had ceased trading for various reasons, and some had been bombed out during the war. In spite of this there were still 155 firms in the London area. I concentrated on these, because what I was firmly interested in was obtaining back-loading for return journeys to the coal fields.

The leaflet was really a blotter. On the blotting paper side was a calendar for the year with the legend alongside, "John Knill and

Columba and *Lucy* in Top Lock, Braunston. Martin and elder son, Tom, on lock side. Alf Best's mother in *Lucy*'s hatches.

Son - Canal Carriers - The name that carries freight any day". It also had a scraper-board drawing *[see top of right-hand pages]* I had done of *Columba*, based on the picture taken at Brentford in 1949. The other side was glossy and carried a map of the canal system, some copy composed for me by Tom Rolt and underneath a broad-side photograph of *Kenelm* emphasising her full 70 foot length. There was on the right-hand side a tear-off portion which could be returned to me in a reply-paid envelope which I also supplied. Of all those firms I contacted, I had replies from only six. From one of these I got my back-loading, but it was not quite what I was expecting.

This reply was from a firm of coal factors in the City of London. I was asked to call to discuss their requirements. They were buying and supplying coal to the Colne Valley Sewage Works in Rickmansworth. The coal was being delivered by BWB craft, but there were problems. Boats had been arriving late and sometimes the coal,which was very fine, had got wet during transport,and then clogged the boilers. Their requirements were for delivery of about 75 to 100 tons per week and the coal was to be picked up from Newdigate, which was for us a very convenient colliery, about two miles from Hawkesbury Stop. I was asked to give a quote for the work. I contacted BWB to find what toll they would charge, sent in my tender and got the job.

The loading was easy. At Newdigate, the boats reversed into the short arm and the coal was shovelled in straight from the rail wagons standing on the track running alongside the canal. Once loaded however, the boats had to be sheeted up. This was fine for *Columba, Kenelm* and *Lucy*, but *Uranus* had no top cloths, as hers had been transferred to *Lucy*. The BWB depot at Bulls Bridge had no sheets available and the only ones I could find at a reasonable price had to come from Leith. They were green canvas, so matched the ones we already had for *Kenelm. Columba* and *Lucy* both had the black tarred variety. There was the inevitable delay in delivery, and we had to hold up our first loading for a short while until we were sure of having the sheets when we needed then. I made a trip to Newdigate specially to deliver them and I well remember how relieved Ron Wilson was when I arrived with the new cloths.

Ron's new engine was working very well indeed. He was very proud of it, as it gave him a slight edge on all other skippers. Alf was also very satisfied with his engine. Few things can lower a boatman's morale more than an engine which plays up all the time, as I knew full well from my own experience. It affects your whole working life from the time you get up in the morning right through until you tie up at night. You often have to give way to other boats at locks; you lose locks that are ready for you. It interferes with everything from cooking meals to doing the washing. In fact, it imposes is worse than trying to coax just a little bit more out of what you feel is (probably correctly) no more than a hunk of scrap iron in the engine room. Now that I was ashore, I could look back with pleasant enthusiasm at memories of *Columba*'s new engine and try to obliterate the awfulness of the experiences with the wretched Bolinder.

Kenelm and *Lucy*

Chapter Fifteen

SELLING UP

The reader may have thought that after four years trading we were set fair for a period of satisfactory results. We had two of the best captains on the canals and the boats in prime condition. Living conditions on board were very good and we had two new engines which could be run at their most economical speeds both from the point of view of wear and tear and fuel consumption.

However, there were two clouds on the horizon, the first to develop slowly as the years went on, only to be overtaken by the second, which then accentuated the first. The first problem was that from the early days we had been under-capitalised. This meant that all improvements had to be paid for out of revenue. This is not of necessity a bad principal in itself, but it is one which could leave you severely stretched at times. It must be emphasised that in the forties and early fifties the attitude of the banks was very different from today. Now they seem to be falling over themselves to loan money, almost pushing it into the hands of small businessmen. There were no Listening Banks or Action Banks; no Visa or Mastercards. Many of the older type of Bank Manager must be turning in their graves at the way their successors carry on! So, towards the end of 1953 we were stretched to our limit with no apparent prospect of help from the bank, the Black Horse being most unwilling.

In the latter part of December 1953 came the second factor - bad weather. The winter was to prove the most severe for a very long time (with the exception of 1947). It was so bad that the canals were frozen over: on the Grand Union for over a month, on the Oxford longer than that. On the Grand Union they had ice-breakers at work, but the Oxford had no such service. I had never seen the operation of ice-breakers before, so I was fascinated to see how it was done. On the Grand Union they were small, flat-decked boats with reinforced bows. Down the centre line of the boat was a rail of about one and a half or two inches thick, and about 14 feet long, supported on stanchions. The boat had a rudder and tiller and was horse-drawn; one, two or three horses according to the thickness of the ice. A team of men, as many as could stand along the length of the bar, stood in equal numbers on either side. The steerer directed a zig-zag course and as he did the gang rolled the boat from side to side by dragging or pushing on the bar, and in this way they could break through ice up to three inches thick. There were steam and diesel ice-breakers, too, but with these there was always the chance of damaging the screw or the propeller shaft.

The ice-breakers needed a certain amount of space to be able to operate, so they were no good in the short pounds or in locks. Here, the only weapons that could be used against the ice were shafts and poles. It was sometimes possible to let water out and the unsupported ice would be attacked with shafts. Even when the ice was broken up, the lock gates could not always be opened properly because large lumps of ice would jam behind them.

The great problem of all this was that the extra work exhausted the boat crews and was also very time consuming. It added hours to the job. A flight like Hatton 21, normally a matter of one and a half hour's work could take nine or ten hours or even longer, and narrow locks like Tardebigge 36 or Wolverhampton 21 were even worse. These incidents might be forgotten by the next week, except as another anecdote for the *Greyhound* or the *Red Lion*, but whilst they were happening they were hell and frustration.

As bad luck would have it, when the freeze started we had just completed delivering a goodly tonnage into the Colne Valley Sewage Works, so they were well stocked up and we were to begin a similar stocking-up over the next few weeks to the Banbury Co-op on the Oxford Canal. The two pairs were just south of Napton when the freeze-up began and they were to be stuck there for six weeks.

But there were other things to distract us. Martin and I had decided to buy a larger and more adaptable car than the Austin 7 we were currently using. We went into Northampton Public Library to look at the magazine Motor. We could not believe our eyes. There, advertised for sale in Manchester, was the car we had both been dreaming about ever since we were married - a twenty horse-power 1923 Rolls Royce station wagon - and its price was £48!

We had previously looked at another Rolls Royce, which had been in the breaker's yard at Cowroast Lock. It had a shooting brake body made by Jack Barclay, the Rolls Royce dealers, and was in fact a much better car than the one in Manchester. When we saw it the rotor was missing, so we had not been able to give it a test run. As I had not had any experience of a Rolls, we had decided not to buy it.

Now we agreed that I should go to Manchester and buy the car that I had seen advertised and so began a very friendly, one might even say loving, relationship with 1923 twenty horse-power Rolls Royces which lasted over 10 years and three different vehicles. Coming back from Manchester, I discovered that the car had suffered from lack of tuning and had a faulty cylinder head. The Rolls had a 14 gallon fuel tank, but in driving it from Manchester to Braunston I emptied the tank three times!

Actually we had gone into the library on the day that Martin went into hospital, this time the Barratt Nursing Home. There, a few days later on 19th January 1954, was born our second son, Jenkyn.

The "new" Rolls turned out to be quite an asset during the freeze-up. I found that my boats were completely frozen in and isolated; the ice around them was from about four to six inches thick. Luckily, although the canals were so bad, the roads were comparatively free of snow and black ice, so I had to use the Rolls as a life-line, ferrying food, milk and paraffin to the two families who were cut off from all other sources of supply.

At last, towards the end of February, the weather improved. We got back into our routine again. After a while, Alf Best began to think about leaving me, to work for the Willow Wren Canal Carrying Company which had just started up. I was lucky enough to replace him with an equally good boatman, Lawrence Grantham. So things were beginning to pick up, but so were the clamourings of the bank. They would not extend my loans, so money for repayment had to be found and the only solution was to sell my boats to the Samuel Barlow Coal Company. The price they offered was £5,750 for the two pairs and, as values went in 1954,

I think that was a fair price.

The agreement with Barlows was four-fold. First, they would buy the four boats. Secondly, they would retain the crews. (It must be remembered that for these boatmen, the boats were home as well as work.) Thirdly, they would take over my commitments to both the Colne Valley Sewage Works and the Banbury Co-operative Society. The fourth condition was that they would employ me as their Boat Manager. I think the worst part of this decision was having to tell Ron Wilson and Lawrence Grantham.

Barlows had at Braunston a Dock Manager, Mr Le Cheminant, who combined his duties with that of Boat Manager, which I was taking over. His wife acted as his typist and secretary. Moving into the main office made things somewhat claustrophobic, so in due course I was provided with an office of my own, a small Banbury concrete structure behind the main office. I enjoyed this new job and felt I was very successful in building up a better feeling amongst all the Barlow crews, including of course, my own ex-crews.

Kenelm, after being sold to Samuel Barlow Coal Company.

I spent time visiting the various boats at several loading and discharging points and en route, both loaded and empty. I always got a cheery greeting, to which I responded in kind. It was whilst returning from one such trip that the Rolls took it into its head to leave the road and finished up as a write-off.

After wondering what I was going to do for a day or two, I discovered actually in Braunston two Rolls Royce coupes for sale. One had a bad engine but a very nice drop-head body by Park Ward. The other had rather a rough body - a Doctor's coupe - but with a good engine. It was also, at £68, the cheaper of the two. So it was the Doctor's coupe that I bought and I had that car for nine years. During that time, it carried me, the family, boat crews, scouts and guides all over the place.

It was now June 1954, and we thought perhaps we might have a holiday. Not long after selling the boats to Barlows I had been ill and suffered a recurrence of a complaint I had first had in 1940. I had been mined and one of the results of this was that I developed a patch of large, painful boils on the back of my neck. The MO at *HMS Wildfire*, Sheerness, did not seem to be able to find a cure for the first week. Then he announced he was to try some medication which had come over in the sick bay of a Free French destroyer, *La Combatante*. It consisted of thin gauze soaked in some kind of oil and packed in layers in a tin. He simply peeled off a layer, placed it on the boils and covered it with a protective dressing. It did the trick. In 10 days the boils had cleared up completely and I was sent off on 14 days sick leave (having already had 14 days survivor's leave after having been blown up).

Now the boils on my neck began to return. Unfortunately I had no idea what the French "gauze and oil" dressing was, so I could not get this to use once more. It appeared that I was going to be laid low again and thought that a holiday might defeat this.

We bought a caravan to tow behind the new Rolls and set off for Borth in Cardigan Bay for a holiday by the sea, the first real holiday we had since we had been married. Martin, Bosun and myself fitted fairly comfortably into the front seat of the Rolls. Behind it was a compartment intended for the doctor's bag and instruments, which was really like a large cot. So the two boys, top to tail, fitted into this space as if it had been made for them. We had a lovely time at Borth, most of which was spent on the beach.

On the way home we stopped to look in at Knill, in Herefordshire, my family home. My direct paternal ancestors had been Lords of the Manor of Knill since at least the twelfth century. There had been a considerable fire at the main house in 1942, and I wanted to see how much of it was still habitable.

Back at work, all went well until the end of September. Then one of Barlow's Ruston engines broke down and I was asked to go to their works to get the spares needed for the repair. The works were 104 miles away in Lincoln and by the time I had received my instructions it was already about 2.30 pm. It was obvious I could not get to Rustons before they closed that evening and would have to stay in Lincoln overnight, ready to be on their doorstep first thing the following morning. It seemed sensible to me to take the caravan to sleep in and given this, there was no reason why I should not take Martin and the boys with me. We found a camp site that evening and next morning, leaving the caravan, I drove the 10 miles to Lincoln and was waiting for Rustons to open at 9 o'clock. I fondly imagined that I would be away by nine-thirty or 10 o'clock at the latest, and having picked up the caravan, could get back to Braunston during the afternoon. But this was not to be.

Picture my dismay when Rustons announced that the firm had been mechanised recently and the "system" could in no way be side-stepped. By the time the request for the parts I wanted had been processed and the parts themselves found and ready for me to take away, it would be at least 3 o'clock. So we kicked our heels for six hours, getting more and more frustrated. By the time we had the parts it was actually after 4 o'clock and we drove straight back home, arriving at about midnight.

When I got back to the yard next morning with the parts, everybody around was looking pretty grim but said nothing; in fact they were very quiet. Then, at eleven-thirty, Stevens, the senior director, turned up. I had always considered him to be rather a pleasant kind of chap. He had handled the buying of the boats, and had met Martin and had always been nice to her and had even on several occasions brought along sweets for the boys - at a time when sweets were still rationed.

Beware of Greeks bearing gifts. He met me in the office, told me that I had been wasting the firm's time and gave me the sack on the spot. We had a very acrimonious quarter of an hour during which I told him exactly what I thought of him and his high-handed methods. I should have had even more to tell him had I known then what I found out later - that this was just a convenient excuse to get rid of me because he wanted the job for his nephew.

Incidentally, the nephew did not last long either, so beware of nepotism, too.

Nowadays there would be a number of ways in which a situation of this kind could be combated, but then there was little I could do except take it lying down. Both the Le Cheminants were very upset about the way in which I was treated, but they could do nothing. In fact, Mr and Mrs Le Cheminant lost their jobs, too, not long afterwards. I talked to Anthony Harvey-Taylor, another small carrier and a member of the NAIWC, but he could not help me and there was nothing that he could do about it, mainly because the major part of his own work was sub-contracting to Barlows, which I could not expect him to jeopardise on my behalf. Since the Aickman activities of 1952, I was no longer a member of the IWA, so could not appeal to them. Finally, when I sold my boats, I automatically ceased to be a member of the National Association of Inland Waterways Carriers, and could make no claim through them direct.

The foreman of the yard at the time was no friend of mine and was a master of tittle-tattle, and I suspect that he had engineered the whole thing. The one bright spot was the loyalty and friendship of most of Barlows boatmen who stood by me, but could do little. Had they supported me openly, they would probably have been sacked too, thus losing both jobs and homes.

Since visiting Knill, we had decided that portions were habitable and we bought the ruins of the house and four and a half acres of land from the owner at the time of our visit, Eddie Davis. We paid him £500 and decided to move in. I had a Bond three-wheeler at this time as well as the Rolls, so we packed everything portable or valuable into the two cars and the caravan. We arranged for all the rest of our belongings to go into store, closed up the house and set off for Knill. Here we made our new home, in the only part of the house still usable at the time, which was once the laundry block.

Joe Hill

During the clearing up and packing I came across my original log for *Columba* and *Uranus* started by Joe Hill. I was so disillusioned and hurt by all that had happened that I destroyed it then and there, which is why I have had to write this book almost entirely from memory.

At that time, I could not conceive how anybody could be even remotely interested in the story of a latter-day Number One.

Martin Knill's account of her first encounter with the canals

ON THE CUT

You know those nice, long narrow painted boats that chug-chug peacefully along the canals through the mild English countryside? There's Dad steering the motor boat, wearing a trilby or a gorblimey; there's Mum steering the butty, perhaps peeling the spuds during the straight stretches; there are a few kids: a little one harnessed to the cabin top and the bigger ones standing beside Dad or poking their heads out of the cabin. Along the towpath a lad or a girl walks or cycles, with a windlass tucked in the belt, on the way to getting the lock ready. Quiet. Peaceful. Dreamy. Effortless. Heaven.

John said, "I want you to have a nice rest. Here's your windlass; you'll need it lock-wheeling". Wally said, "Any tea mashed?"

The butty was brave with roses and castles, shining brass and cupboards that opened and turned into tables or beds. A cream-coloured stove stood by the door. A pair of bright, telescoping candlesticks cunningly wrought in brass shot out from the wall and entangled themselves in my hair. The chimney had three brass bands round it and a brass chain to keep it anchored to the cabin top, while the gaily painted water can was tied on with another brass chain. There was a brass port-hole and the cabin doors had brass insets on the outside to reflect the light to oncoming boats. The stern end of the cabin had brass plates for the same purpose. It all looked lovely and so clean....

There were white cotton-line turks heads round the rudder (sorry, I mean 'ellum) and other twists with fancy rosettes; beautiful ropework everywhere, and all so white and clean. I wondered how they did it. I soon learnt.

The forward part of the cabin had a door which opened on to the "back-end". This name shook me, as no doubt it does you. It is the after end of the hold called the "bottom". From end to end the boat is 70ft long and the cabin takes up nine of the feet. In width, it is 7ft so that, in the cabin, by the time you have taken off the bit that slopes to the sharp end aft and the space for the stove, cupboards, lockers and side-bed, space is rather restricted. All very bright and polished though.

My first job was to go and draw. I looked bright and intelligent and hoped for elucidation. John steered the stern of the butty to the canal side where a bridgehole brought a stone apron halfway into the middle of the cut, smiled nicely, said "Don't forget your windlass" and levered me ashore. I walked fast. Wally tooted and made "hurry up" signs. I ran, thinking the lock was round the corner. It wasn't, so I walked. The motor came in sight and Wally tooted again. In this way I ran about three miles towards Birmingham; a hundred yards had always been my limit. When the lock came into sight I breathed a sigh of relief, turning rapidly to dismay. What did I do now? One mustn't waste water. On the other hand, the lock had to be ready for the boats to go in. I tried to work out the system, but a boater called George came to the rescue. The lock was emptied, the downstream gates opened, the sluices dropped, the boats came in "breasted up". The downstream gates were closed, the top sluices opened, the lock filled. The top gates were opened, the boats went out leaving me upon the towpath evidently destined to run the rest of the way to Birmingham.

All this might sound simple, but the lock gates are tree trunks pivoted in mediaeval fashion so that all one's strength is needed to shift them. The sluices are raised by winding up the paddles with the windlass. There seemed to be a great dearth of grease except on the part of the paddles where there was no friction, and on one's hands. I was quite exhausted, in spite of George, Wally and John all helping. When I say "helping", I really mean that they did all the work; it wore me out just to look at it.

At about 2.30, John said "You should have a lesson in steering". I thought this a good idea: far better than wrestling with tree trunks and scrap iron. I waited for my lesson. "Quick, take the tiller", said John. I rushed up to find him leaping lightly ashore at a bridge hole. Apart from a brief interlude for lunch, wash and supper, I steered until 12.30 that night. I complained of the dark. Nobody cared. I complained that I couldn't see. Nobody cared. To John and Wally it was simple. There was the water, and there were the banks. All you had to do was to keep in the water and not go up on the banks. The motor had a light, even if it was 140 feet away and out of sight round the bends. Steering was hard work - going round corners you needed your feet, hands and weight and then had to hurl yourself in the opposite direction to keep the stern of the boat away from the shore. When both ends of a boat 70 feet long and carrying 32 tons of zinc have to be steered by a tiller and a gi-normous rudder, I mean 'ellum, the still and contemplative side of boating seems far, far away.

The great advantage of being left alone on the butty is that you can sing all the songs you know at the top of your voice. If your voice is like mine, you will appreciate this rare opportunity. The men on the motor couldn't hear. Anybody else would be left behind. The pewter and Indian ink of the water and shore had their own noises: the plopping of the voles and the sound of the wash among the reeds. The night journeys were by far the best. Certainly I went aground, or "stemmed-up". I was so busy looking at the outline of the tree tops on a sharp bend before a crooked bridge that I forgot the foot of the trees. Pity. Wally was covered in mud before he got me off. I knew he was making shooting signs at me: giving me both barrels, blowing the smoke away and pitching the gun into the cut, but I didn't care. The skill of the operation impressed me enormously. If they left me to steer in the dark before I'd had my lesson, it was their fault. John appeared unmoved. No catastrophe ever frenzied him. The engine broke down repeatedly, but he remained unruffled and oilier than ever. When I bashed into the lock-side doing a clumsy breasting-up, Wally it was who got infuriated. So did I, of course: the impression I wished to make wasn't a dent in the boat.

We got to Birmingham and unloaded. It was late night and I enjoyed steering the butty through the narrow waterways in the city, past the great wharves and factories with their flaring lights. The fairway was singularly cluttered with other craft, the steep sides of the buildings towering up in a most unbashworthy way. I had never been to Brum before and I was quite entertained to come to it in so unusual a way. We tied up at the depot at Samson Road.

The next trip was to Coventry for coal. I had never been to Coventry before. We travelled empty and the butty was snubbed up short against the stern of the motor. This was dull as the only steering required was to keep the stern away from the bridge holes. However, there was the eternal brass to polish, the cabin tops and sides to wash, the rope work to clean, the socks to wash and mend and the shirts. There was also the daily 7lbs of spuds to peel for the three, of us. Never a dull moment. And of course the locks - twenty one of them in one place. All John would say as we faced them the second time was, "You have to do Hatton 21 in the right spirit". How true: how very true. One certainly had neither body nor mind at the end of them.

For losing weight and eating like a horse; for hard work and long hours in the sun, wind and rain; for exercise and time for thought; for comradeship and the interest of other boats and other boaters; for a helping hand and ready sympathy; for getting down to the basic simplicities of life, give me the "Cut". For the glow of pride when the lock-keeper, watching the boats move in, says "Quite like old times, seeing a well-kept pair of boats"; for lovely physical tiredness followed by instant sleep; for the first cup of tea in the early morning with the mist rising from the water, there's nothing like the Narrow Boats and the Inland Waterways.

Best of all was starting off as The Visitor, and ending as The Second Mate.

Footnote from Sir John Knill:

This account, written by my late wife, Martin, was not found until I was sorting through her papers shortly after she passed away.

A Poem by Ray White

THE BOATMAN'S RETURN

HAWKESBURY JUNCTION 1986

It's back again, and home again, and here at Sutton Stop
I've come to seek familiar things that modern folk's forgot.
It must be sixteen years (or more) since lorries boating killed,
And up and down our waterways the motor boats were stilled.
In basins, arms and dockyards, their rusting skeletons lie,
Reminders of a way of life that took so long to die.

Now, round the bend to Tushes Bridge, the towpath stretches bare,
But in my mind those ghostly pairs still wait for orders there.
At weekends, or at holiday times, they made a stirring sight,
Their brasses bright and shining, their cratch-strings dazzling white.
Their cabin-sides proclaimed they came from companies old and new
Like 'Waterway' and"Willow Wren', to name the biggest two.
And, further back, come 'Barlows', both 'Limited' and 'S.E.',
Then 'John Knills', 'Cowpars', 'Joshers' - (the famous FMC).

Now, turning to the Coventry side, where *Friendship* used to tie,
The pleasure craft lie stem to stern, where coal trains once went by
Across the cut on wooden bridge - that too has gone to burn -
One day, perhaps, the roads will be redundant in their turn.

The monstrous concrete cooling towers that stood at 'Longford Light'
Were blown up several years ago, and weeds now mark the site.

Between the 'Cov' and Oxford cuts, an office used to stand,
From which each morn' the captains came, their orders in their hands.
The building still is there, tis true, but where is Mr Shaw?
Or dear Miss Doreen Edwards, the boatman's friend of yore?

I turn around and face the north, where houses used to be.
Across the Coventry stop-place, a wondrous sight I see.
The pumping engine chimney, and engine-house still stand.
For once they've left them standing, restored by caring hand.

A Pity 'bout the footbridge, which for many years has stood
And now it is 'unsafe to use' - it's only made of wood.

Of Fieldings and the 'Salvo', there is no trace today,
Salvation Army folk were praised along the waterway.
And many a boatman's child (new born) was christened by them, too.
And any time that trouble struck, they know just what to do.

So now towards the pub I turn, the centre of our lives.
The *Greyhound* was a 'home from home', for boatmen and their wives
Alas, it has been 'Modernised' (it never had a bar),
And boating folk feel strangers now - its patrons come by car.
And gone too, is the little shop, where boat-wives spent their pay,
Buying enough of this and that to last till settling day.
Our friendly, Mrs Nelson, 'Rowie' and Nuala too
No longer serve folks beer and crisps - it's not the pub I knew.

I think of dear Joe Skinner, the last of that long crew
Of owner-boatmen (Number Ones), and of the *Friendship* too.
Preserved at Ellesmere Port she lies, for modern folk to see.
But I remember meeting her, when bound for Banbury.
Joe's faithful mule called 'Dolly', but she took sick and died,
So Joe and Rose tied up their boat along the Coventry side.

I think that I have seen enough of Sutton Stop today
I find it too depressing now the boats have gone away.
The boating life held lots of fun - and lots of hard work too.
Those folks today who glamorise it often have no clue
Of what it's like to drive a horse all day in pouring rain
Then wake up in the morning - and do it all again.
I'll keep my private memories, and dream what might have been –
(If England wasn't lorry mad) - a bright new boating scene.